Semiotics of Subtitling

Zoé de Linde and Neil Kay

St JEROME

PUBLISHING

First published 1999 by

St. Jerome Publishing
2 Maple Road West, Brooklands
Manchester, M23 9HH, United Kingdom
Fax +44 161 905 3498
ken@stjeromepublishing.com

Reprinted 2009

ISBN 10: 1-900650-18-5
ISBN 13: 978-1-900650-18-2

Printed and bound in Great Britain by
TJI Digital, Padstow, Cornwall

Cover design by Steve Fieldhouse, Oldham, UK

British Library Cataloguing in Publication Data
A catalogue record of this book is available from the British Library.

Contents

List of Tables

List of Figures

Acknowledgements

Many friends and colleagues have contributed to this book. We are particularly grateful to Jim Kyle, Tom Troscianko, Brian Stollery, Kirsten Malmkjær, Robert Baker, Catherine Neary and Helen Stone, with special thanks to Christen and Josephine de Linde. Our editor, Mona Baker, has also made many detailed and helpful comments on the draft version.

We are especially grateful to the staff and former students of the Centre for Deaf Studies, University of Bristol, who participated in the research featured in this book. Finally, we wish to thank the Social and Economic Research Council for their financial support (award number: R00429334097) and the BBC, ITV and Channel Four for their permission to reproduce and quote from broadcast material.

Preface

A growing amount of information is being presented in audio-visual form, through traditional media like television and cinema, and newer technologies such as the Internet and Digital TV. In future, this trend looks set to continue with increased use of computers and network facilities.

All forms of audio-visual media present a combination of sound and visual information. Access to such information depends on people being fully receptive to both channels. There are many instances where this is not the case. In television and cinema, for example, a film is often produced in one language which has to be subsequently translated into the native languages of 'secondary' audiences. Similarly, the sound elements of television programmes have to be subtitled for deaf and hard-of-hearing viewers. The dynamic multimedia environment of television and film means that neither of these practices is solely linguistic as the transfer of dialogue into written form is strongly influenced by the structure and semiotics of a film or television programme.

This book is an analysis of the processes and influences involved in subtitling for deaf and hard-of-hearing viewers, including: the condensing and transformation of dialogue between spoken and written language modes; the conversion of other significant features of a soundtrack into graphic form; the reading capacities and viewing strategies of deaf viewers, and the way in which subtitle features influence viewing behaviour. Many of these elements are also involved in other types of audio-visual language transfer, including interlingual subtitling, making much of the material covered widely relevant. Moreover, the monolingual aspect of intralingual subtitling allows many of these elements to be perceived quite transparently, without risk of any effects being 'lost in translation'.

Besides making an academic contribution to research issues, this study also has a strong pragmatic agenda. Audio-visual mediums such as television are becoming increasingly significant for people generally (Gambier 1996), but they are of utmost importance to deaf and hard-of-hearing people for whom subtitling is an essential information facility. In this respect, the efficacy of the medium is particularly important and it is hoped that the analyses conducted will have an impact on practical prescriptive questions as well as highlighting areas of further research.

In order to appreciate the complexities in subtitling, it is necessary to take full account of the dynamic integrated environment: each subtitle is realised within a particular audio-visual context, styled according to the conventions of speech and writing, and edited with an eye on the structure of a film and the reading characteristics of target viewers. Understanding these processes requires drawing on knowledge from a range of subject areas as well as an appreciation of both technical and semiotic issues. However, as noted above, because of the differences between inter- and intralingual subtitling there has been little research addressing all aspects of the medium. In general, intralingual subtitling has been studied from a technical pragmatic perspective as a communication aid; interlingual subtitling, on the other hand, has tended to be analysed linguistically as a form of translation.

This study aims to combine both these approaches: analysing the content of subtitles through linguistic theory while examining viewing behaviour by empirical observation. By adopting this kind of holistic approach, it is hoped that the book will set new ground in the study of subtitling revealing many issues which arise from a full appreciation of the integrated audio-visual context. In this respect the issues covered should be of interest to practitioners and researchers working in a variety of fields, including linguistics, translation, the media, psychology and film studies.

Chapter One: Subtitling and Audio-visual Language Transfer

1.1 The context of subtitling

As noted in the preface, there are two distinct types of subtitling: intralingual subtitling (for deaf and hard-of-hearing people) and interlingual subtitling (for foreign language films). The distinction between them stems from the different requirements of deaf and hearing viewers. While it is often assumed that interlingual subtitles serve all viewers adequately, in practice this is not the case. Interlingual subtitle rates are too high for many deaf viewers and only the linguistic elements of a soundtrack are transferred. Importantly, the soundtrack of a film or TV programme carries two sources of information: linguistic information derived from the content and phonetics of a dialogue, and non-speech information: sounds, etc, which also contribute to the overall meaning of a programme. Interlingual subtitles transfer the meaning of utterances while relying on the remainder of the soundtrack, including phonetic cues, to carry the full meaning of a film sequence. As intralingual subtitles are addressed to deaf viewers, many of these elements also have to be transferred.

It is therefore difficult to speak of a theory of subtitling as, on the one hand, the practitioners of interlingual subtitling have tended to be translators and on the other, the roots of subtitling for deaf and hard-of-hearing people lie in industry and assistive technology (Norwood 1988; Thorn 1990), as intralingual subtitles grew from the need to provide a written account of what was said on screen.

However, despite their apparent differences both types of subtitling have strong common elements: they take place in the same audio-visual context; they both involve a conversion of spoken dialogue into written text, and in both forms the amount of dialogue has to be reduced to meet the technical conditions of the medium and the reading capacities of viewers. In inter- and intralingual subtitling language is being transferred between distinct linguistic systems, between two separate languages and/ or between different modes of a single language, while functioning interdependently with another, visual, semiotic system. In this sense, the term used in the title of this chapter and adopted from now on, *audio-visual language transfer*, captures the processes common to both types as well as to other related practices such as dubbing.

1.2 A typology of audio-visual language transfer

Of the various forms of audio-visual language transfer, a principal distinction is often made between subtitling and dubbing. Both forms have distinct characteristics making them more or less acceptable to a non-homogenous set of target viewers. In terms of 'national' preferences, a decision on which method to choose is often based more on economic considerations than cultural characteristics. Countries with relatively smaller numbers of viewers, and consequently limited levels of investment and production, tend to favour subtitling, it being the cheaper method. In contrast, larger countries usually favour dubbing as, even though it is the more expensive alternative, it can potentially attract larger numbers of viewers.

In a European context, this broadly explains the following situation. Subtitling is the favoured form in Portugal, Greece, Wales, Holland, Luxembourg, Ireland, and parts of Belgium. Dubbing is the preferred alternative in France, Germany, Britain, Spain and Italy (Gambier 1996). However, individual programmes attract different sections of a national viewing audience which will also influence the choice between subtitling and dubbing. Both subtitling and dubbing are also associated with many related subtypes:

- *Simultaneous subtitling* in real time, for live interviews and news broadcasts, etc.
- *Simultaneous interpretation* taking three possible forms:
  a) live and often with summarizing as, for example, on the radio
  b) pre-edited, much like a *voice-over*
  c) in long distance two-way television interviews or at teleconferences
- *Voice-over*, characterized by a translation reasonably faithful to the original and quasi-synchronous.
- *Narration*, where a text is read by a professional reader, actor or journalist, where the text is prepared, translated and sometimes condensed in advance and where the original dialogue is evanescent. The form can be contrasted with a *voice-over* which attempts to be approximately simultaneous.
- A *Commentary*, whereby a programme is adapted to suit a new audience with the possibility of information being added and taken away. Synchronization is made with the images rather than with the original dialogue, which is erased.
  Both *Narration* and *Commentary* (commonly used for children's programmes, documentaries and promotional videos) are like a combination of translation and interpretation because of the reductions (compressions and omissions) and other alterations made to the original soundtrack and their orality. Between *dubbing* and *commentary*, there are many diverse forms of oral transfer.
- *Multilingual diffusion*, where a viewer chooses from a selection of sound-tracks the one in his or her desired language through Teletext.
- *Surtitles*, sometimes used in operas and theatres whereby a translated text is projected or run across a screen above the stage.
- *Simultaneous translation*, a form of translation *à vue*. It is produced from either a script, subtitles or from running text, realized in a foreign language. It is found at some film festivals. Without a script, it would be closer to a *voice-over*.
  (translated from Gambier 1996)

Many forms are a mixture of features found in subtitling and dubbing. For example, Gambier characterizes *subtitling* as a kind of simultaneous written interpretation while describing *voice-over* as something approaching oral subtitling. In this sense, the special features of the medium have given rise to new modes of discourse, adopted in respect of the genre of film or TV programme, economic considerations and the intended viewers.

Common to all audio-visual language transfer is the requirement of synchronicity between audio and visual channels; this is crucial in dubbing where there must be a match between labial consonants and vowel openings but also important in more interpretative modes such as *voice-over,* which must still be quasi-synchronous. With subtitling, the coordination of sound and image is made more complex with the addition of a textual component, further illustrating the semiotic interplay in all forms of audio-visual language transfer.

1.3   Analysis of subtitling

As noted above, the differences between intralingual and interlingual subtitling stem principally from their target viewers: deaf and hard-of-hearing people and non-native language users, respectively. Their different requirements impose different objectives on the two forms of subtitling. The objective in intralingual subtitling is to substitute the dialogue and other important features of a soundtrack by a written representation, while in interlingual subtitling the objective is to achieve something approaching translation equivalence.

While the two types can be distinguished in this way, both still encounter the essential differences between spoken and written language. Take for example the following sequence from Quentin Taratino's film *Pulp Fiction*:

Intralingual subtitles	Interlingual subtitles
Three tomatoes are walking down the street. Papa, mama and baby tomato. Baby tomato starts lagging behind. Papa tomato gets really angry ... goes back and squishes him. Says "Ketchup"	La famille citron se ballade. Papa, maman et bébé citron. Bébé citron est à la traine. Papa citron se met en boule ... le rejoint et l'écrabouille en disant "presse-toi ... citron pressé"

Table 1: Comparison of Intra- and Interlingual Subtitles

Both sets of subtitles derive from the same dialogue and have to reproduce a homophonic pun on 'catch up/ Ketchup'. In intralingual subtitling, this is achieved by writing in the least common word thus hoping to activate both alternatives simultaneously. In interlingual subtitling, the task is perhaps further complicated by the pun having to be reproduced within a different phonetic system. In the above case, this causes a content shift but as the two senses are not precisely homophonic they are both made explicit.

1.4   Linguistic background

Interlingual subtitling differs from text translation in a number of ways: there are additional visual and audio components including a residual oral soundtrack; there is a switch from oral to written language and, finally, there are obligatory omissions in the source dialogue. In view of these differences, the question is sometimes posed whether subtitling or 'screen translation' can be viewed as a form of translation. The view which one takes must partly depend on one's definition of translation. For example, Luyken (1991) cites Newmark's statement that "translation must ... replace a message and/ or a statement in one language by the same message and/ or statement in another language" as grounds for excluding subtitling, since only the language component is actually being replaced in a message which comprises 'the whole audio-visual opus'. However, other definitions of translation are more suggestive of the linguistic processes involved in subtitling, for example, Toury's definition (1980), based on the concept of relevant features.

> Translation equivalence occurs when a SL and a TL text ... are relatable to ... the same relevant features ...
> Relevance... (1) is to be regarded as an abbreviation for "relevant *for* something" or "relevant *from* a certain point of view"..;
> (2) ... since a text comprises various "features" on various levels, ... all of which are ... relevant for the totality of the text, the opposition relevant-irrelevant should be conceived of as polar, rather than binary, and we should speak in terms of *hierarchies of relevance*, rather than of absolute relevance.
> (Toury 1980:37-38).

The various "features" Toury refers to include elements such as 'sounds, letters, word meanings, syntactic patterns, textual segments and principles of segmentation' (Toury 1980:38).

In subtitling it is self-evident that only the linguistic element of an audio-visual 'text' is transferred but in its altered form must still relate to the source utterance, thereby warranting the same kind of analysis as a translation, including the introduction of concepts such as *relevance* and *equivalence*.

In a similar way, these concepts can also be applied to intralingual subtitling as it entails a transfer of information between oral and written language modes involving a reconstitution of the meaning of an utterance. In fact, the transfer of information between oral and written systems is perhaps more conspicuous in intralingual subtitling since deaf people do not receive any indicators from the soundtrack, thus the informative value of suprasegmental phonetic features, such as intonation, have to be partly expressed in writing (see chapter two). Furthermore, in both forms the transfer of information does not simply involve omitting elements of dialogue but a reconstitution of information with respect to the different functions of speech and writing.

> ... in its core functions, writing is not anchored in the here-and-now. The particular conditions that obtain at the time of writing are some distance from the writer both in time and space; so much of the message that is contained in the rhythm and timber of speech would simply be irrelevant.
> (Halliday 1985:32)

This description is generally applicable, whilst the degree of 'orality' in writing often varies between languages.

> Certain prosodic features are accidental properties of the particular language: for example, some of the meanings that are expressed by intonation in English are expressed by particles in Vietnamese or in German; so in those languages these meanings get written down, whereas in English they do not.
> (Halliday 1985:32).

A further feature related to the transfer of meaning between speech and language is the *dilemma of accuracy* as a balance has to be struck between the clarity of a particular utterance and its stylistic function. For example, there are many elements of speech which at first sight appear superfluous and consequently omittable when converted into written form, for example *actually, well, you know*, etc, but these may in fact be integral to a character's style of spoken discourse. In this sense, the transfer of language mode imposes complex choices on the part of a subtitler, in an attempt to respect the features of both spoken and written modes.

In addition to, and tied up with the transformation from speech to written form, are the necessary omissions in the dialogue. Fast spoken words can rarely be transcribed into two (or possibly three) lines of written text. Thus the dialogue has to be condensed, which in turn means selecting particular features of the source text to be omitted, by straight deletion or reductive paraphrasing.

Drawing on Halliday's system of language functions, Kovačič (1992) suggests that the choice of omissions is based on the function of their language sign. The least omittable elements are carriers of the representative function, as:

- They are surface representations of the underlying propositional relations;
- They are not supported by the film or television medium to the same extent that elements with personal or cohesive functions are: personal functions combine with the visual and audio information coming from the screen, and cohesion is strengthened by the continuing story on the screen. (Kovačič 1992:250)

Kovačič (1994) later modifies this notion by drawing on Relevance Theory (Sperber and Wilson 1986) to rationalize a larger variety of omissions, since a similar interpersonal feature may appear in two different contexts and may be strongly relevant in one of them but almost incidental in another:

> When the subtitler is short for space, he/she evaluates the relative relevance of individual segments of a given message. Relying on the viewers' ability to apply adequate cognitive schemata or frames and to draw on either previous information in the story or their general knowledge of the world, the subtitler leaves out the part of the message he/she considers the least relevant for understanding the message in question, for perceiving the atmosphere of a situation or the relationship among the participants involved, and eventually for the general understanding and reception of the story.
> (Kovačič 1994:250)

Particular examples of such relevance-dictated omissions might include co-extensive and co-intensive sequential strings, expansion strings (causal, resultative, explanatory, anticipatory, adversative) and dispensable modifications.

A theory based on a communicative approach to translation is supported by Reid (1991), who views subtitling as 'communicative translation par excellence'; it is much less concerned with the words of the speaker than with the intention of what the speaker wants to say.

Many deletions can be accounted for by the principle of relevance but there are difficulties in using it as a strong explanatory tool. The main weaknesses in the theory have been pointed out before (Levinson 1989): it is not easily formalised and has weak predictive power. At the root of these weaknesses are the three cognitive principles themselves (processing effort, contextual effect, and relevance) which are difficult to estimate precisely in any situation. In practice, any description of a context tends to be both subjective and extremely difficult to delimit. In film, for instance, the context of an utterance might be considered to range over the whole narrative.

Taking an example cited by Kovačič, relevance theory is used to explain the substitution of a longer element by a shorter one which bears an 'interpretative resemblance' to the first:

(1) I woke up *three minutes ago*.
(2) *Pravkar* sem se zbudila. [*I just* woke].

This provides a reasonable explanation for the omission within the context of the utterance, but the specific quantification in (1) may have been more widely significant, typifying a character trait, for example, or signifying an ironic marking of time.

Defining the context of an utterance tends to be more difficult, on the whole, with more narrative forms of discourse. Thus, while the explanatory power of Relevance Theory is often illustrated by excerpts from everyday conversation, its application to narrative forms, including many films and TV programmes, tends to be more problematic as artistic texts propose to be as 'interpretative' as 'communicative', in the sense of not simply conveying messages but activating ideas and themes. Under these circumstances, the 'interpretative resemblance' between two phrases is more open to negotiation. Therefore, while omissions might be broadly considered to be relevance dictated, in practice the subtitler encounters much of the same complexities as faced by a translator.

1.5 The audio-visual dimension

The main conditions of subtitling stem from the integration of text, sound and image, the reading capabilities of target viewers, and the restrictions which these two factors place on space and time. These restrictions place special demands on a subtitler, meaning that the transfer of dialogue into written captions is not a straight-forward matter of transcribing a lexical sequence.

1.5.1 Spatial restrictions

Reading speeds and screen space differ between cinema and television but, in general, subtitles generally take up a maximum of two lines, containing no more than forty characters. The actual space taken up by each subtitle is also a function of the original utterance and, in the case of interlingual subtitling, the comparative properties of source and target languages.

For example, the abbreviated genitive form 's' in English; the replacement of prepositions by suffixes in Hungarian (Ignotus 1972:306); the elision of short vowels and the use of superscripts in Arabic and Urdu, all help to conserve space on screen. Other features however may have the opposite effect. Hungarian for example makes no distinction between the pronouns 'he' and 'she'. Both are denoted by the same third person singular pronoun 'ó' (pronounced like the French 'eux'). This may seem like an economical feature, but as Ignotus has pointed out, it is not always so:

> It is most inconvenient for instance for the translators of romantic fiction; there can be no *'he enfolded her hand between his'*, it must be something like *'The man enfolded the woman's hand between the man's own.'*
> (Ignotus 1972:304-305, as quoted in Minchinton 1993:4.10).

1.5.2 Temporal restrictions

The restriction on time derives from the need for synchronicity and the reading speeds of viewers. Luyken et al. (1991) suggest that average reading speeds for hearing viewers hover around 150 to 180 words per minute. There have been many difficulties establishing reading speeds for deaf viewers, with no universally accepted figures. Kyle and Pollen (1985) suggest that deaf people's reading abilities are close to those of nine-year-old hearing children.

Even with the above information, many complications arise with the multimedia environment, making it difficult to transfer these statistics. Reading speeds not only vary according to the quantity and complexity of linguistic information in subtitles, but also in relation to the type of visual information on screen at any given moment.

Minchinton (1993) has recounted how the genre of film can affect viewers' reading patterns:

> [With an 'I love you' story] viewers need not read many of the titles; they know the story, they guess the dialogue, they blink down at the sub-titles for confirmation, they photograph them rather than read them ... Crime stories and espionage tales give translators and viewers a harder time. The subtitles have to be read if the subsequent action is to be understood.
> (Minchinton 1993:4.14-4.15)

There are many other cases with similar effects, where the dynamic information on screen is significant to the point that subtitles have to be restricted to essential static information, leaving a viewer's eye free to roam the image. For example, when a character's attention is distracted from a group conversation towards another character, it is only necessary to indicate that the conversation is continuing, leaving viewers time to focus on the important information in the image.

Reading speeds are also affected by the subject matter of a programme or film. Minchinton (1993) remarks that "viewers rarely complain of the speed of detailed titles, ... perhaps because the story is exciting and viewers' reading speeds are boosted" (Minchinton 1993:4.15).

These examples highlight the difficulties in establishing reading speeds and thus standardized subtitle presentation rates. Actual subtitle presentation rates vary from company to company but in general correspond to roughly three seconds per line. Depending on programme content, this may be interpreted as about three seconds for a full text line, five to six seconds for two lines, and eight seconds for three lines.

1.5.3 Synchronization

A film or TV programme is a combination of visual images and an audio soundtrack including dialogue. The transformation of the dialogue into written subtitles must be carried out with respect to the relations between all these components. As well as a spatial balance between subtitle and image, there must also be a precise synchronization of image and subtitle; a procedure which is more than a matter of approximate timing as both systems are semiotically related.

This relationship is perhaps best illustrated in comic situations where linguistic expressions must co-ordinate with the visual image. A recent poignant example from British television was part of a live commentary on the FA cup final, inside the press box above Wembley football stadium. Terry Venables (ex-England manager), who had recently lost a court case to Alan Sugar (famous entrepreneur), was offered a cup of tea by Clive Anderson (comedian) and asked *"Milk, no sugar ?"*. Here the subtitle had to combine perfectly with the shot changes in order to capture the interplay of textual and visual features. Most programmes will carry a stream of other examples, particularly instances of conversational dialogue which has to be strictly coordinated when several people are speaking simultaneously.

1.6   Summary

This chapter has described the context of subtitling and introduced the main elements of the audio-visual environment. It is hoped that in doing so it has illustrated the common ground between inter- and intralingual subtitling and other forms of audio-visual language transfer. The following chapter focuses on intralingual subtitling, describing the issues concerning the effectiveness of the medium and the related research carried out for this book.

Chapter Two: Intralingual Subtitling

2.1   Introduction

Since the introduction of speech to motion pictures (c.1930) deaf (and foreign language) viewers have had to rely on various methods of representation to understand the source dialogue. One of the most common methods of display available to deaf and hard-of-hearing viewers is subtitling.

The term 'Sub-title' derives from the term for a subordinate or additional title of a literary work (*OED* 1989). In the history of cinema (between 1895 to c.1930) the term was initially used for the text or 'intertitles' of silent movies, which were cut into the film at various strategic points as a narrative aid. Both deaf and hearing viewers had the same access to films (although there was still the issue of whether deaf viewers could read the 'intertitles').

Problems arose with the introduction of 'talkies' (sound films) and the consequent removal of intertitles in the 1930's, which shut the door of the film industry on the deaf community. In 1947, Emerson Romero, a deaf Cuban actor who had performed in several silent films, purchased a number of films, inserted his own inter-title cards for the dialogue, and rented them out to a number of deaf organizations. While this method lengthened the film considerably, it led to efforts in 1950 by the Conference of Executives of American Schools for the Deaf to set up a similar library of films, this time with the subtitles superimposed on the film scenes (Van Cleve 1987).

New problems emerged in the wake of television. Unlike film, television was broadcast widely into the homes of deaf and hearing people. Studies by HRB Singer (Norwood 1988) had shown that although a significant number of hearing viewers reacted positively to subtitles, broadcasters were reluctant to risk even the slightest loss of advertising revenue as a result of reduced ratings. No clear figures existed for the numbers of hard-of-hearing people who would be viewing subtitled programmes, and networks felt that the ten per cent of hearing viewers who reacted unfavourably to captioned television in the study would be larger than the deaf population (Norwood 1988; Thorn 1990).

A solution to these problems came with the invention of closed subtitles, i.e. subtitles which were hidden within the broadcast signal and visible only to people who had a special decoding device. In the U.S.A. transmission of closed captions was implemented through the designation of line 21. This means subtitles appear on line 21 of the Vertical Blanking Interval (VBI) – the black horizontal bar between individual television images – at a range of about two characters per frame, or 60 characters per second. Similar systems were set up in France and Britain with the installation of ANTIOPE 1983 (Acquisition Numérique et Télévisualisation d'Image organisées en Pages d'Ecriture) and TELETEXT in 1976.

Today many developed countries have supplemented programmes subtitled for the deaf with other programmes interpreted in sign language. As with subtitles the provision of 'signed' programmes is not likely to increase until a system is devised to conceal the signed presentation within the broadcasting signal. With the advent of digital television this could soon become a reality.

Table 2 shows the extent of films broadcast for deaf and hard-of-hearing viewers today. The table seems to indicate quite a favourable situation with a large number of films subtitled for the deaf. However, the picture is deceptive. Most films involving interlingual subtitling are not tailored to the demands of deaf viewers. They do not compensate for the loss of *all* sounds (including non-verbal noises) nor are they adjusted to viewer reading abilities. Turn down the volume of an interlingual subtitled film and you will experience some of the frustrations endured

	Subtitled programmes * Mainly interlingual subtitles	Programmes with sign language pw = per week
Belgium Fl	Numerous *	News flash
Belgium Fr	Numerous *	Daily news
Canada En	75% of news, 250hrs (pw)	Parliament in session (with ST, French SL)
Canada Fr	90hrs (pw)	Daily news & 1 religious programme
Czech Rep.	10hrs (pw)	Daily news & 1 programme (per month)
Denmark	Numerous *	Daily news & 2 programmes (1pw & 1 per month)
Finland	Numerous *	Daily news
France	10%	Daily news, news flash & 1 programme (pw)
GB	30% (BBC), 25% (CH4)	Daily news & 3 programmes (1 pw & 2 per month)
Germany	Numerous *	Daily news
Israel	Most films *	Daily news
Norway	50%	News flash, magazine & 1 programme (per month)
Spain	1 programme	Daily news
Sweden	All adult programmes	News flash & magazine
Switzerland	Most films *	Daily news & 1 programme
USA	Numerous *	Daily news

Table 2: Intralingual Subtitled Programmes and Programmes with Signing in a Range of Countries (Adapted from EBU Conference Notes 1994).

by deaf viewers: confusion over who is speaking the subtitled words; puzzlement as to why, for example, there is a sudden change of human behaviour (e.g. the panic stricken face of someone who hears a murderer's footsteps); misunderstanding due to an overlapping subtitle across a shot change.

Research by Woll (1991) has suggested that subtitling on its own is not the preferred method of language transfer for deaf and hard-of-hearing viewers. Out of 57 subjects only 2% expressed a preference for subtitling *alone* on mainstream programmes.

Deaf Translators & Subtitles	35
Deaf Translators, Hearing Interpreters & Subtitles	27
Deaf Translators Only	16
Hearing Interpreters & Subtitles	11
Hearing Interpreters Only	5
Deaf Translators & Hearing Interpreters	4
Subtitles Only	2

Table 3: Communication Mode Preferences: Mainstream Programmes (%)
(Woll 1991)

It is interesting to note that when watching deaf programmes 27% of deaf viewers stated that they do not watch subtitles when a deaf person is signing, but do watch them when a hearing person is speaking or signing. This seems to be because hearing signers are often less easy to understand than deaf signers.

> When deaf signers appear they are generally originating their own linguistic content, while when interpreters appear they are generally operating both under time and content constraints. This is likely to make their signing less intelligible than that of deaf signers, even when their formal language skills are equivalent.
> (Woll 1991:11).

A much larger study involving approximately 2500 participants (Kyle 1992) revealed that when faced with a film with no subtitles 22% of viewers would switch off, 38% would try to guess, 29% would try to lip-read and 36% would try to use their hearing aids. This choice varied according to deaf status, with deaf signers more likely to switch off or to guess while hard-of-hearing people were more likely to try to listen with their hearing aids (Kyle 1992).

2.2   Importance of subtitling

The importance of subtitling for deaf and hard-of-hearing people cannot be overstated. In Europe it is estimated that 1,100,000 people are profoundly deaf and 80,000,000 are hard-of-hearing (European Commission 1995). A recent survey carried out in Britain (Gunter 1993) identified television as being the main source of world news.

The principal means for deaf and hard-of-hearing viewers to access information on television is through subtitles. British broadcasters have recognized the need for extensive subtitled coverage by seeking to match the requirements imposed on the new Channel 3 (ITV) franchise-holders in the 1990 Broadcasting Act to subtitle at least 50% of all analogue programmes by the end of 1998. The 1996 Broadcasting Act extends this requirement to all digital programmes licensed by the ITC (ITC 1997).

2.3   Technical description of subtitling

Intralingual subtitling is a process aimed at reproducing, in a written form, the dialogue of a television programme to enable deaf and hard-of-hearing people to access spoken information. As will be shown, it is rarely possible to produce a verbatim transcription of a spoken dialogue due to a shortage of space and time. The aim rather is to present the nearest equivalent meaning in written form. There are many variations in the production of subtitles but in Britain the essential stages are as follows (ITC-URL 1997):

The subtitler receives a videotape of a television programme to be subtitled. They play the tape and make a transcription of all utterances and sound-effects. This is saved as a data file on a computer. The subtitler then divides the text into blocks of 'subtitles'. Specially developed software is used to display each subtitle over the image of the programme on the television screen. The subtitler positions and colours the subtitles according to the respective speakers.

All videotapes are lined with magnetic time codes (e.g. Burnt-In Time Codes BITC, or Vertical Interval Time Codes VITC). These time codes act as counters, displaying the time elapsed since the start of the tape. This information is crucial as it identifies the position of each frame and enables the subtitler to position the subtitles accurately.

The subtitler plays the videotape a second time to record the start and finish of each line of dialogue. These markings act as 'in' and 'out' cues to each subtitle. Software records the cues by reading the time codes on the tape. This enables accurate display and removal times of each subtitle. A small adjustment is usually made to compensate for the time lapse between hearing the speech and setting the cue. The tape is now ready for editing.

As the average reading speed of adult viewers is estimated at 66% of the average speaking speed (ITC-URL 1997), each subtitle has to be reduced by approximately a third. This is the main reason why there cannot be verbatim subtitles. The reading times for children's programmes are even longer – roughly double that of adults (ITC-URL 1997).

The subtitler replays the television programme. Subtitles now appear in sequence with the videotape as all the 'in' and 'out' cues have been matched with the time codes. Final checks are made on spelling, punctuation and overall meaning before the tape is ready for broadcasting.

The final stage in the subtitle process is the viewers' selection of programmes with subtitles. In Britain this is carried out by calling up page 888 on their teletext television.

2.3.1 Deaf and hard-of-hearing viewers
The deaf community is made up of two distinct groups; those who are born deaf, and those who acquire a hearing loss later in life. Both groups differ in outlook and needs. The first group's main method of communication is sign language and their ability to use subtitles may be hampered by relatively low reading levels. The second group, people with acquired hearing loss, are more likely to have had an education within the hearing community and will consequently have average reading speeds. The vast majority of this group become deaf in their 50's and 60's (Davies 1989). Figure 1 clearly shows that the oldest age groups have greatest difficulty in viewing TV.

Reading ability is thought to be one of the main factors in the comprehension of subtitles (Areson and Dowaliby 1985) (c.f. chapter three). The difference between conventional reading and reading subtitles on screen has been summed up by Baker (1987):

•   The speed of reading is not under the reader's control. Subtitles appear and then disappear, whether you are ready or not.

- The reader is being asked to do two different things at once: read and watch television pictures.

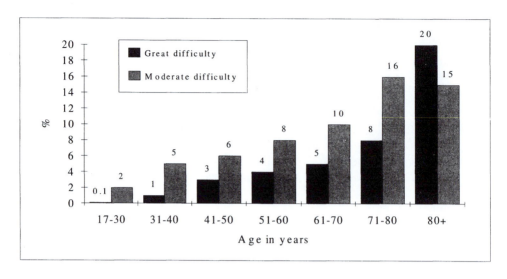

Figure 1: Difficulty in Television Viewing (Kyle 1992)

As mentioned previously, average reading speeds differ between deaf and hard-of-hearing groups. In the case of people who have been born deaf, hearing loss is an effective predictor of reading ability. In young deaf people this has been measured as equivalent to the reading ability of an average nine year old (Kyle and Pullen 1985). Deaf people are at a disadvantage on two accounts; not only are their reading levels lower than average but their breadth of knowledge is also restricted by a limited access to information throughout their education. Research into text reading speeds suggests that as many as 84% of deaf school children will not be able to read at the rate of speech on television (Shroyer and Birch 1980).

In contrast, there is no evidence to suggest that the reading ability of people who have acquired hearing loss is adversely affected. This means that there is an unusually large range of reading abilities among deaf and hard-of-hearing viewers and that the normal speed of subtitling is likely to be problematic for many deaf people (Kyle 1992).

2.4   Subtitling for deaf and hard-of-hearing viewers

When analyzing intralingual subtitling, it is impossible to separate the integrated semiotic systems (both audio and visual information) from the requirements of deaf and hard-of-hearing viewers. As the audio track is not completely available it must be compensated for by some other semiotic system which is accessible.

The audio track carries two distinct forms of information: phonological information which contributes linguistically to the dialogue, and non-speech information which typically consists of meaningful and non-meaningful sounds. These have to be compensated for within the constraints of the medium.

2.4.1   Representing the phonological component

Subtitlers employ many features to indicate a wide range of elements related to the sound component of the moving picture.

2.4.1.1   Emphasis and phrasing

The simplest way of indicating an increase in volume is by using capital letters; emphasis of individual words can be achieved by a change in colour. Subtle nuances of phrasing are difficult to deal with effectively, but special techniques can be used. For example the 'line-break' technique, whereby one line is broken into two, is sometimes used to indicate hesitation and afterthought (BBC 1994):

No ...
... But I don't dislike him.

This dynamic method of simulating speech timing and phrasing can be very effective, but if overdone can produce a rather jerky presentation (c.f. chapter eight).

2.4.1.2   Tone of voice

There are no adequate resources for representing tone of voice in intralingual subtitling. Deaf people necessarily make use of facial expressions in one-to-one communication, and this is a further important reason for allowing the viewer time to read each subtitle and to watch the associated image of the speaker, if on screen. The devices mentioned above for expressing emphasis and phrasing can provide additional help. Where tone of voice is particularly critical to meaning and the facial expression is an inadequate indicator, the use of (!) and (?) immediately following speech can indicate sarcasm and irony as shown below (although they do not indicate which word is being emphasized):

No, no. You're not late (!)

2.4.1.3   Accents and foreign languages

Where accents and foreign languages contribute to viewers' appreciation of a film they have to be represented in the subtitles. For example in a drama or comedy where a character's accent is crucial to the plot, the subtitles have to establish this feature. However, at other times, a phonetic representation of a speaker's foreign or regional accent may slow up the reading process and possibly ridicule the speaker. For example, to represent the flavour of a Cockney dialect, any characteristic vocabulary or sentence constructions such as "caffs", "missus" and "ain'ts" might be included, but it would be inappropriate to consistently use non-standard spellings. Where the dialogue is insufficient to capture the flavour of an overseas/regional speaker – as with American accents to, say, British viewers – labels have to be used (BBC 1994):

AMERICAN ACCENT:
TV is a medium because it is neither
rare nor well done.

2.4.1.4   Humour

Humour, perhaps more than any other feature, highlights the interplay between the three semiotic systems of the medium. Some jokes depend on the synchronicity of word and image, others on the interplay between spoken and written language. Homophones, for example, cause particular problems for deaf viewers as the oral component is not recoverable from the sound track. One way of preserving both meanings in a pun is to spell out the word according to the less obvious meaning. For example, consider again the pun cited in the last chapter from Tarantino's film *Pulp Fiction*:

Three tomatoes are walking down the street.
Papa, mama and baby tomato.
Baby tomato starts lagging behind.
Papa tomato gets really angry...
goes back and squishes him. Says "Ketchup".

By substituting the words 'catch up' for 'Ketchup' the subtitler can highlight orthographically the play on words.

2.4.2   Subtitling the non-verbal component

2.4.2.1   Sound effects
Even the most accurate representation of a sound is likely not be as evocative as the sound itself. However, where sounds influence a character's actions or contribute to the atmosphere of a programme it is important that they are transcribed. Thus though

BLOODCURDLING SCREAM

will not curdle the blood, the viewer at least knows the intensity of the sound that SCREAM alone would not convey (Baker et al. 1984).

Sounds which need not be transcribed are those which are indicated visibly on screen, e.g. a shot of a clapping audience invariably needs no APPLAUSE subtitle.

Some subtitlers question whether it is useful to subtitle sounds that deaf people have never heard. However as noted before, a typical set of 'deaf' viewers is made up of a variety of people. They range from people who may have only partial hearing loss or who have lost their hearing later on in life and who still retain 'images' of the sound, to 'viewers' who are more or less dependent on visual clues to access the dialogue and other sound elements.

2.4.2.2   Music
Although it would be difficult to represent the tune of a song, the title and lyrics can be subtitled. This is particularly important if the lyrics are connected to the story line, as in opera and some pop music programmes. Lyrics are often distinguished from speech subtitles by means of a # sign. Provision of an occasional subtitle for mood music, if it is significant to the plot, can be very effective (BBC 1994).

2.4.3   Subtitling in a dynamic medium
The dynamic aspect of films and television programmes is particularly important in subtitling. As subtitles substitute for dialogue, they must retain the same coordination with speakers and other visual features.

2.4.3.1   Locating and identifying speakers
Locating and identifying a speaker becomes problematic in the following situations, when:

* characters are talking off screen
* a narrator is speaking
* a group of people are talking
* there are unknown off-screen voices
* characters are moving on screen, or a group of people are talking against a shot change.

Various methods are used to overcome the problem of coordinating dialogue with characters. These include the use of a variety of fonts; punctuation e.g. >>; use of name tags; strategic placement of subtitles, and colour. Research into colour at Southampton University (Baker et al. 1984) suggested the order of legibility is white, yellow, cyan and green. Magenta, red and blue should be avoided (Baker et al. 1984). Excess colour coding is thought to be inadvisable as it could potentially lead to greater confusion.

The use of right-left placement to locate a speaker can become problematic if there is a change in the camera angle. For example, while a group of people remain stationary, a change in camera angle may make the person on the right look as if s/he is on the left.

2.4.3.2   Timing and synchronization

While the need for synchronicity between oral utterance and written text underpins both types of subtitling, it is perhaps most acute in intralingual subtitling where considerable frustration is felt by deaf and hard-of-hearing viewers when faced with silent moving mouths. Previous eye-movement research (Baker 1982) suggests that deaf and hard-of-hearing viewers make use of facial cues on screen to direct their gaze to the subtitle area (c.f. chapter eight). If no subtitle is present, the resulting 'false alarm' causes considerable irritation. A later extension of the study (Baker et al. 1984) revealed the following reaction:

* change of subtitle detected
* read subtitle
* scan picture until another subtitle change is detected.

The same 'rules' of synchronization are also thought to apply in the case of off-camera speakers and even off-screen narrators since deaf and hard-of-hearing viewers with a certain amount of residual hearing make use of auditory cues to direct their attention to subtitles.

Research on interlingual subtitling has suggested that the disappearance of each subtitle should coincide roughly with the end of the corresponding speech segment, since those remaining too long on screen are likely to be re-read by viewers (d'Ydewalle 1987). It is also thought that where possible, consecutive subtitles should not directly over-write one another, rather they should be separated by brief pauses allowing the viewer time to register that a new subtitle has arrived.

2.4.3.3   Leading and lagging

'Leading' and 'Lagging' refer to the lapse in time between the appearance of a subtitle and the start of a corresponding speech segment. If a subtitle precedes the speech the delay is referred to as lead time, if a subtitle follows speech it is referred to as lag time.

The target point for speech/subtitle synchronization is thought to be at naturally occurring pauses in speech-sentence boundaries, or changes of scene. However there are many cases where this is neither practical or applicable. Research has shown that for programmes consisting mainly of monologues perfect synchronization is not an absolute necessity and delays of up to six seconds do not affect information retention (Baker et al. 1984). The same is true of leading subtitles (provided that the first word of the subtitle is synchronized with the corresponding speech). In this respect, the type of film or TV programme, or discourse segment, affects the presentation of subtitles, although little research has gone into analyzing the variations between genres. In intralingual subtitling, it is also the case that some viewers use subtitles to support heard speech and will require closer synchronization of leading subtitles.

2.4.3.4   Shot changes

In addition to the requirement for subtitle-speech synchronization, there are certain other aspects of the image frame which influence subtitle presentation. Subtitles that are allowed to over-run shot changes can cause considerable perceptual confusion. Eye movement research (Baker 1982) has suggested that shot changes which occur while a subtitle is being shown cause viewers to return to the beginning of a partially read subtitle and start re-reading. In practice, the frequency and speed of shot changes in many programmes makes it very difficult to overcome this problem.

2.4.3.5   The need for research

The previous sections have described the context and technical features of intralingual subtitling. Although guidelines have been written on how to produce effective subtitles, few research studies have been carried out to investigate the many complex aspects of the medium.

A pilot study was conducted on viewing behaviour at Southampton University involving a small number of participants (Baker et al. 1984). Results were inconclusive as the analysis of eye movements was based on only two participants and there were difficulties in obtaining usable recordings. A further investigation of re-reading against a background of shot changes also involved a limited number of participants.

A more recent research study focused on legibility factors including lag time, colour and add-ons (Kyle 1992). In the case of lag time (the time between speech and the appearance of a corresponding subtitle) results indicated that there was no effect on the retention of story content until the delay reached over four seconds, when the retention of programmes with dramatic content was affected. For programmes involving mainly monologues or commentaries, lag time effects, even at six seconds, were not thought to be great. Colour was considered by viewers to be an important and helpful part of subtitles but no effects on story retention were detected. The same was also true of the use of add-on lines, although viewers were less likely to notice their presence (Kyle 1992).

The other important issue has been verbatim subtitling, the achievement of which ultimately depends on the speed at which utterances are delivered in relation to viewers' reading and comprehension speeds. There has been no direct examination of these factors. Research conducted by Baker et al. (1984) was carried out at a time when many deaf and hard-of-hearing people did not have a television set in their homes and were relatively new to the idea of subtitles. The two subjects in the eye-movement experiment differed markedly in their ability to cope with text speed – one being able to deal with very fast text while the other found it impossible. As Baker (1987) noted himself, a more sophisticated set of viewers would probably be available for another study in ten years time.

While these studies have provided some insights into viewing behaviour as affected by particular subtitle features, there has been very little examination of the linguistic aspects of subtitling in relation to the transfer of meaning and the effects of editing.

2.5   Proposed research

While looking at elements common to both types of subtitling, the research carried out in this book is focused on intralingual subtitles for deaf and hard-of-hearing viewers. As illustrated, much of the complexity of subtitling derives from the integrated multimedia environment of television and film. Moreover, intralingual subtitling has to cater for the needs of viewers whose own methods of communication are extremely diverse, ranging from sound-based approaches through residual hearing and lip-reading, to visual approaches such as sign language.

An attempt is made in the following chapters to take account of all factors relating to the medium and viewers, including an analysis of the linguistic properties of subtitles vis-à-vis film content and reading behaviour. This inevitably means drawing on knowledge from a range of disciplines, including Psychology, Deaf Studies, Film Studies, and Linguistics.

2.5.1   Analysis of subtitling standards
A pre-requisite of such a study is the establishment of basic measures of subtitle characteristics: speech and subtitle rates; the amount and frequency of shot changes; lead and lag times, etc. At present, no measures of current broadcast subtitles on British terrestrial television have been recorded or analyzed systematically. One of the primary concerns of this study is therefore to establish such measures. These are important not only to determine differences between programme types (e.g. between programmes subtitled for adults and children) but also to serve as a base line measure for further research.

2.5.2   Transfer of language
Subtitles integrate with oral, visual and audio information. In contrast to these forms, subtitles are not conceptualized at the time of film production. Rather, they are later additions which must combine with the audio-visual make-up of the source film.

When oral dialogue is substituted by textual discourse (i.e. subtitles) the overall structure of the film narrative is changed. Verbal and visual information can no longer be processed simultaneously; instead, they have to be processed in succession (i.e. the viewer can no longer monitor the image and the dialogue at the same time. Their attention now has to be divided between processing the image and reading the subtitles).

The substitution of oral discourse by a visual textual discourse changes the nature and subsequently the role of the verbal discourse (c.f. chapter four). In contrast to speech, written discourse has its own lexico-syntactic patterns (Halliday 1994): simpler sentence structures and a higher density of content words. These linguistic differences inevitably have implications for the semantic and pragmatic content of the verbal message (c.f. chapter four) yet so far little research has touched on the effects of this transformation.

As well as a transformation in discourse mode, the required reduction in the amount of text imposes selective judgements on a subtitler. This process has been analyzed and rationalized through linguistic theory but the specific effects of particular categories of omissions on readability are also highly significant. A key question is to what extent   cohesive features of language affect comprehension? Cohesion plays an important role in making relationships between entities in a text explicit. Often these devices are omitted when condensing oral dialogue into subtitle text (de Linde 1995). Thus, although the aim is to simplify the text, omission of cohesive devices may lead to greater difficulties in comprehension. This problem may be compounded by the fact that subtitles are displayed only for brief moments, giving viewers no recourse to previous text while having to process dual references between text and image (c.f. chapter four).

2.5.3 Reading characteristics of viewers
In addition to linguistic and film features, how subtitles are ultimately received is also determined by the reading characteristics of viewers.

A large number of variables affect reading: familiarity with the subject or topic of a text, interest and exposure to a type of discourse, etc. Many of these variables are relevant to deaf and hearing people alike. Where both groups differ significantly is in their fundamental use of language. Deaf people are a linguistically diverse group. They differ in their degree of hearing loss, in their first language (which may be either sign or spoken) and in their reading strategies and abilities (Gregory 1996). This study focuses on the range of cognitive strategies used by deaf people to read written text (c.f. chapter three) and the implications of these strategies for subtitling. Four methods of recoding are considered: articulatory codes, dactylic, visual, and no intermediary coding.

2.5.4 *Analysis of viewing behaviour*
As eye-movements are a critical factor in determining how well a viewer participates in a subtitled programme, more research is required on the key behavioural features, i.e. where the eyes focus in relation to the entire screen and how this is reflected in the take up of information and programme enjoyment.

Previous studies of viewing behaviour have relied on viewers' comments or the results of comprehension tests. Viewers have either participated in national surveys using current broadcast subtitles or been asked their views on controlled subtitle formats (c.f. chapter five). This study adopts a relatively new approach, combining traditional methods of assessment with detailed eye-movement studies. A record of how the eyes move during silent viewing provides a valuable insight into how specific characteristics of subtitles affect reading.

2.6   Summary of objectives

The overall objective of this book is to examine the core aspects of subtitled television: notably, the semiotics of subtitles and film with respect to the reading characteristics and viewing behaviour of deaf and hard-of-hearing viewers. The analysis is complemented by a practical assessment of subtitling standards on British terrestrial television in order to establish differences between programme types and to serve as a baseline measure for further research.

As noted in the initial chapter, many studies have focused on the technical conditions of intralingual subtitling while relatively little research has been carried out on linguistic features. This study attempts to adopt a holistic approach, using linguistic theory in combination with eye-movement analysis in the hope of gaining further insights into the effect and reception of subtitles. In analyzing intralingual subtitles in such a manner it is hoped that the study will contribute to a better understanding of subtitling in general and, in particular, subtitling for deaf and hard-of-hearing people.

Chapter Three: Reading Characteristics of Deaf and Hard-of-hearing Viewers

3.1 Introduction

In addition to adapting to the original structure of a film, (c.f. chapter four), subtitles must also reflect the reading capacities of viewers. Thus, estimated reading speeds influence the length of captions and their display time.

As noted in the previous chapter, reading speeds are not fixed. They may vary depending on the level of interest a person has in a subject or topic or their degree of familiarity with a particular programme. For example, a regular viewer of *EastEnders* is more likely read the subtitles quicker than when they watched the soap-opera for the first time. Subtitle reading speeds are also affected by the need to process two channels of information simultaneously, both subtitle and screen image. This also affects the amount of text that can be displayed.

While all these factors apply to deaf and hearing viewers alike, in general deaf people do not read written text as quickly as hearing people. This results in longer subtitle display times and the ommission of more words from the dialogue.

The main distinction between deaf and hearing peoples' reading is thought to rest with the cognitive mechanisms associated with 'inner speech', which aid the conversion of text into meaning. These mechanisms are employed by hearing people but apparently not by the deaf. How, then, do deaf people read?

Rather than the use of inner speech, a number of other cognitive strategies are available to deaf people. Each involves recoding written text into an intermediate representation. The various methods are analyzed and compared in the following sections with reference to subtitling.

The purpose of this chapter is to examine how deaf people read in order to contribute to a better understanding of the subtitle medium. This entails analyzing the behavioural features associated with inner speech and the alternative mechanisms available to deaf people. By investigating these aspects of reading, many of the less understood difficulties facing deaf viewers can also be identified, including those relating to the differences between British Sign Language and English.

3.2 The concept of inner speech

Inner speech has long been considered an important aspect of reading (Huey 1908). However, different views exist over what exactly constitutes inner speech and what precise role it has to play in text comprehension (Rayner and Pollatsek 1989).

Inner speech manifests itself in two ways: through activity in the speech tract (either muscle movement or articulatory processes) otherwise known as *subvocalization*, and by mental representations of speech which give rise to the experience of hearing sounds, known as *phonological coding* (Rayner and Pollatsek 1989). The relationship between these two behavioural features is still somewhat unclear. In this chapter, the generic term 'inner speech' will be used to refer to both unless stated otherwise.

Three basic techniques have been used to study inner speech in proficient readers:

- Measuring the muscular movement in the speech tract during reading (through *Electromyographic recording*) (Garrity 1977, Taylor 1983).

- Determining the extent of interference in reading when the use of speech is made impossible (through *concurrent vocalization*) (Besner et al. 1987, Slowiaczek and Clifton 1980).
- Investigating whether the sound properties of a text (such as homophony and phonemic similarity) affect reading (Treiman and Hirsh-Pasek 1983, Van Ordern 1987).

The results of experiments based on these methods are discussed below.

3.2.1 *Electromyographic recording (EMG)*

Studies in EMG activity have provided some useful data regarding subvocalization in reading. Less skilled readers exhibit more EMG activity than skilled readers (Edfeldt 1960, McGuigan and Bailey 1969) and the rate of subvocalization appears to increase as text becomes more difficult (Edfeldt 1960, Sokolov 1972). Whilst subvocalization is thought to be directly linked to speech activity (Garrity 1977) it is unclear what happens to reading comprehension when subvocalization is suppressed. Despite the difficulties in assessing whether subvocalization has been eliminated or not (McGuigan 1971, Taylor 1983), it is thought that when it is eliminated and subjects are faced with a difficult text, reading comprehension suffers (Hardyck and Petrinovich 1970).

3.2.2 *Concurrent vocalization*

Studies of inner speech interference based on concurrent articulatory activity have been inconclusive. This is partly due to the complex nature of inner speech. Even though a particular reading of a text may not be vocalized it may be phonologically coded, i.e. when reading a text it is quite possible for a person to hear the words whilst uttering something else. Secondly, subtle interference effects may be missed because they may lie in the vocalization task which cannot easily be measured (Rayner and Pollatsek 1989).

Studies suggest that although inner speech interference in text comprehension cannot be ruled out, it is generally thought that both phonological coding and subvocalization are involved in short-term memory processes (Kleiman 1975). Studies recording little interference indicate that phonological coding is more important than subvocalization in identifying the meaning of words (Levy 1978, Slowiaczek and Clifton 1980).

More recent studies by Besner et al (1987) suggest that oral interference tasks mainly have an effect on the storage and manipulation of inner speech rather than on its initial production from text. Whether concurrent vocal activity has an effect on the production of inner speech from written text is still unknown (Rayner and Pollatsek 1989).

3.2.3 *Homophonic reading*

Studies in homophonic reading support the notion that inner speech is significant in the reading process. Most studies confirm that the speed and/or accuracy of silent reading is influenced by the sounds of words (Treiman and Hirsh-Pasek 1983, Treiman et al. 1981, Treiman et al. 1983, Baron et al. 1980, Van Ordern 1987). For example, when presented with two sentences where one word has been replaced in each, in the first by a similar sounding word and in the second by a different sounding word, subjects find it harder to reject the former (Treiman et al. 1983). Likewise, sentences containing a series of words that rhyme or alliterate (tongue-twisters) are more difficult to read both silently and aloud (Ayres 1984, Haber and Haber 1982). The effects of such exercises are commonly attributed to post-lexical processing in working memory, although the picture remains unclear.

3.3   Deaf readers

The studies discussed above have provided substantial evidence on the importance of speech recoding in processing text. The following sections address the question of what happens when a person cannot engage in speech recoding? Do deaf readers, in fact, 'read' (alphabetic) text?

Studies comparing deaf and hearing peoples' reading capacities suggest that deaf people are able to read alphabetic text but less proficiently. A study carried out in the USA on 17,000 deaf students found that just over 25% of a group of 19-year-olds were functionally literate. Reading comprehension, measured by the paragraph-meaning subtest of the Standard Achievement Test, peaked at age 19 for hearing subjects and at age 4 for deaf subjects (Di Francesca 1971). A similar study examining nearly 7000 deaf students recorded a median score equivalent to grade level 4.5 for deaf people aged 20/plus (Trybus & Karchmer 1977).

In England and Wales a survey carried out on nearly all 15 to 16.5 year-olds attending special schools measured the median reading age, on the basis of a sentence completion test, to be equivalent to 9 year-old hearing children (Kyle and Pullen 1985). Few studies have examined the reading skills of deaf people after they have left school, but according to one report comprehension remains low, although vocabulary does improve (Hammermeister 1971).

The difference between deaf and hearing peoples, reading capacities is hardly surprising. To begin with, deaf people do not learn English through the same educational channels and they are unable to benefit from the alphabetic writing system as they do not have full access to the sound structure of English.

Secondly, those people born deaf have a different knowledge of English syntax (Russell et al. 1976, Quigley et al. 1977). Indeed, for the majority of deaf people, their native language is not English but British Sign Language (BSL) which differs from English in a number of important ways. BSL has its own lexicon of signs and borrowed words, morphemic devices for generating complex signs from simple ones, and grammatical rules for combining signs into sentences (Kyle and Woll 1985, Stokoe 1995). These features differ markedly from those of English. Thus, many deaf people not only have to process a language without any phonological component but also one which differs markedly from the language which they 'speak'. This situation perhaps explains the findings of Woll (1991) that the preferred method of audio-visual language transfer among deaf and hard-of-hearing viewers is a combination of subtitles and signing by deaf translators (c.f. chapter two).

It is important to note that research has also shown that some profoundly deaf people read proficiently. For example, a study conducted in England and Wales found that on completion of formal education 4.5% of young deaf people were able to read at a level commensurate with their age (Conrad 1977). Such 'good readers' are less common among those with a profound hearing loss than among those with considerable residual hearing (Conrad 1977, Di Francesca 1971), perhaps indicating the importance of a phonological resource. However, amongst people who are profoundly deaf, those with deaf parents have been found to be better readers than those with hearing parents (Buchanan et al. 1973, Trybus and Karchmer 1977), which also seems to emphasize the importance of effective communication at an early age.

3.4   Recoding strategies among the deaf

Studies of deaf readers indicate that phonological coding may not occur as they read (Locke 1978, Quinn 1981, Treiman and Hirsh-Pasek 1983). As deaf peoples' first language is not oral, this is perhaps to be expected and immediately begs the question of which mediating system, if any, deaf people use in going from written text to meaning? Four alternatives have been examined:

- Articulatory codes
- Dactylic (fingerspelling)
- Sign language
- No coding

3.4.1 Articulatory codes

Even profoundly deaf people have some access to the phonological system of English (or the relevant spoken language) via articulation and lip-reading. Although lip-reading has its limitations due to the difficulty in deciphering similarly pronounced consonants such as 'b' and 'p' (c.f. cued speech), it does enable some deaf people to make judgements about rhyme (Dodd and Hermelin 1977) and the spelling of novel words (Dodd 1980). Therefore, it is possible that some deaf people recode written text into some form of articulatory code based on their own manner of articulation and/or that of others.

Research has found that some profoundly deaf people use articulatory codes in short-term memory tasks (Conrad 1979), displaying behavioural patterns similar to those shown by hearing people: confusion over similar sounding letters and reduced performance with lists of phonologically similar items, relative to control lists. However, the extent of articulatory recoding by deaf people is relatively low even among those in oral schools (Conrad 1972, 1979) and while it may assist in memory and word identification, it does not take advantage of the natural language of deaf people.

3.4.2 Dactylic (fingerspelling)

Another option available to deaf people is the recoding of alphabetic text into fingerspelling. Fingerspelling is a manual system in which each letter of the alphabet is represented by a particular handshape. Thus the word:

> *IF*

is recoded as follows:

Figure 2: 'If' in British Sign Language

Fingerspelling is a unique aspect of BSL in that it is a manual version of written English as opposed to being made up of signs. It is used for a number of reasons: to introduce new concepts which do not yet have a sign e.g. 'cyberspace'; for representing proper names, and for some very common signs such as 'if' (Sutton-Spence 1995).

While fingerspelling is not officially part of sign language, most deaf people are able to fingerspell their signed lexis. Therefore, they would be able to recode written text into fingerspelling. This has been the case in experiments involving short term memory tasks where deaf participants have recoded visually presented letters into fingerspelled representations (Locke 1970, 1971). The one-to-one relation between alphabetic letters and fingerspelled handshapes makes the translation from one system to the other a straightforward one, which may encourage recoding by this technique. Research suggests that deaf children improve in printed word identification when fingerspelling those words that are familiar to them in their fingerspelled lexis (Hirsh-Pasek 1981).

3.4.3 Sign language

A third option for deaf readers is to recode printed alphabetic words into their sign equivalents. As sign language is the first language of most deaf people, sign coding may be the easiest method to process alphabetic text. Research suggests that this technique is used as an aid to short-term memory. In a series of experiments involving deaf participants, intrusion errors were frequently caused by signs bearing a visual resemblance to another sign which had been previously presented (Bellugi and Klima 1974, 1975). For example, when the ASL (American Sign Language) sign NOON was presented,

Figure 3: 'Noon' in American Sign Language

written (and signed) intrusion errors made by deaf ASL signers included the response TREE (pictures taken from Humphries et al. 1980).

Figure 4: 'Tree' in American Sign Language

In another study using a continuous recognition paradigm, it was discovered that a false-recognition effect frequently occured with formationally similar signs, i.e. deaf participants falsely recognized new signs which were similar to previously presented signs more frequently than they falsely recognized control signs (Frumkin and Anisfeld 1977). Similarly, experiments involving short-term serial recall tasks showed that recall accuracy in congenitally deaf participants was significantly lower on cherologically related lists than on both phonologically related lists and control lists (Shand 1982).

Experiments exploring all alternative means of mediation (articulatory, dactylic, visual, no coding) have shown converging results. In a phrase evaluation task with homophonic words and tongue-twisters, deaf participants did not experience as much confusion with homophones as hearing participants, suggesting that there was less articulatory recoding. There was also little evidence to support the hypothesis that a majority of deaf participants recoded printed words into fingerspelling. However, participants had considerable difficulty with sentences containing similar signs ('hand-twisters') indicating that there was a marked degree of recoding into sign (Treiman and Hirsh-Pasek 1983).

3.4.4 No recoding

A final option is that deaf readers may not recode at all. Evidence for this has come from research on the effects of orthography on inner speech. Observation of non-alphabetic systems with weak grapheme-phoneme relations (such as Chinese) has led to suggestions that, in some cases, readers are able to go directly from print to meaning without recourse to inner speech. However, there are two problems with this hypothesis.

Firstly, it is partly based on an assumption that the lexicon is always activated directly from visual presentation, yet non-alphabetic systems are seldom purely logographic, some characters being based on sound (Martin 1972). Secondly, it is assumed that no benefit is derived from the post-lexical coding of information into sound codes to aid short-term or working memory (Pollatsek and Rayner 1989).

It is clear that speech recoding does occur among Chinese readers because they make confusion errors in short-term memory tasks between phonologically similar sounding words and letters (Tzeng et al. 1977, Tzeng and Hung 1980, Yik 1978). However, further research has indicated that speech recoding occurs less frequently among Chinese readers than among English readers (Treiman et al. 1981). In addition, studies in Japanese show that there is less concurrent articulatory activity when reading Kanji than when reading Kana (Kimura 1984, Kimura and Bryant 1983).

Therefore, it appears that once logographic characters are learned, they are phonetically recoded in working memory (Erickson et al. 1977). Although it is possible that inner speech may be somewhat less important in logographic systems such as Chinese and Japanese Kanji than in largely phonetic languages like English (Seidenberg 1985), the fact that a language can be processed without a phonetic component is clearly exemplified by sign language.

3.5   The role of recoding in comprehension

There are many theories on the role of recoding in comprehension. With respect to hearing people, there are two alternatives: either they recode printed text into a phonological form or they derive meaning directly from print without any mediation at all. It has been proposed that recoding into phonological form has several advantages: it facilitates comprehension (Mattingly 1972) and working memory and aids printed word identification.

For the deaf reader, the issue is more complex. Four possible recoding strategies have been discussed, none of which appear to be as efficient as phonological recoding (Treiman and Hirsh-Pasek 1983).

Articulatory recoding is most similar to phonological recoding in the sense that it allows deaf readers to take advantage of English spelling, which could potentially aid English word identification. However, as spoken English is not deaf peoples' primary language, articulatory recoding would probably not aid comprehension to the same degree as in the case of native English speakers.

The second option for deaf people is recoding into fingerspelling. Although, again, it is not officially a language, most deaf people are believed to have a sizeable fingerspelling vocabulary (Locke 1970). A fingerspelling strategy could therefore offer some comprehension advantage. Fingerspelling has also been reported to be an effective memory code for deaf people (Locke 1970). It may also prove useful in word identification due to the unique letter-handshape correspondence.

The third option is recoding into sign language. Sign language is the primary communication system of most deaf people. A strategy of recoding into sign would therefore seem an obvious choice, particularly since working in a primary language has advantages for short-term memory and comprehension. Research has suggested that sign is an effective memory code (Shand 1982), yet there is no regular relationship between the form of a printed word and the form of a corresponding sign. Thus, again, it may only provide a limited aid to word identification.

3.6   Summary

In summary, some deaf readers appear to consult their native sign language when reading alphabetic text. The comprehension and memory advantages provided by their primary language probably weigh heavily on this choice of recoding strategy (Treiman and Hirsh-Pasek 1983). Although sign language bears no direct relation to print, access to sign language (possibly in an 'inner' form) does appear to assist reading. In addition, articulatory and dactylic coding are also available, presenting the possibility of a combination of strategies. The possibility of no recoding has also been discussed with reference to research studies on logographic systems.

Although it would be dangerous to stress any strong implications for subtitled television, research has shown that more than one method of language recoding takes place among deaf viewers, and that each method of recoding differs in the degree to which it facilitates comprehension, working memory and printed word identification. As the subtitle medium includes both verbal and visual information, it would be particularly interesting to study the effect of each recoding method on the processing of subtitles. Chapter eight describes a preliminary investigation into how deaf and hearing viewers respond to different types of subtitles, but more knowledge needs to be acquired about the reading/viewing process before further experiments can be conducted to examine the relationship between different recoding strategies and subtitled television.

The discussion of reading strategies in this chapter has highlighted the linguistic diversity within the group of people at which subtitled television is aimed. Among people born deaf, there are varying levels of residual hearing which may influence their recoding strategy and therefore have an effect on reading rates. But in the case of people with acquired hearing loss, reading rates are likely to be similar to those of hearing people.

In the light of this diversity, it would be difficult to select an ideal subtitle rate for all viewers. At present, only one rate is possible, but with the introduction of digital television it would be feasible, technically, to encode more than one set of subtitles with a programme.

Chapter Four: The Integration of Text and Film

4.1   Introduction

Subtitles are a mixture of speech and writing in the sense that they represent oral utterances in discrete written captions with the transitoriness of speech. The transformation of dialogue into subtitles is influenced by three main factors: captions must integrate with the existing material and semiotic structure of a film; speech has to be presented in an altered written mode and subtitles must be designed so as to take account of viewers' reading capacities (c.f. chapter three).

The purpose of this chapter is to analyze these factors to further develop an understanding of the medium. The following sections study text and film elements of subtitling and their integration in film and television, highlighting issues of meaning and design, as well as areas requiring further research.

4.2   Textual features

The transformation of television dialogue into subtitles involves a switch from spoken to written language mode and a necessary reduction in the amount of dialogue. The latter requirement is clearly well known to the point where subtitling is often seen as a form of text editing. Less obvious perhaps are the stylistic and structural differences between speech and writing which also influence the transformation and the way that any omissions affect the meaning of an utterance.

The following sections examine the two key textual features affected by the transformation process: language style and text cohesion.

4.2.1 Language style

The differences between speech and writing have been well documented (Biber 1988, Halliday 1985, Halliday and Hasan 1976, Nunan 1993). There have been two main approaches to the study of each language mode. The first approach is to characterize speech and writing according to situational parameters (e.g. formal/informal, restricted/elaborate). The second approach is to use linguistic features to describe the characteristic aspects of each mode (e.g. nominal/verbal, structurally simple/structurally complex). Both approaches have also been combined by identifying sets of co-occuring linguistic features in each form and grouping them according to specific dimensions (Biber 1988).

The problem with the latter research for the purposes of this study is that there is no single dimension that can be used to describe the differences between speech and writing. Rather, the reader is provided with a set of dimensions which not only differ according to modalities but also according to different genres within each modality. In order to identify structural changes between spoken and written text it is necessary to focus on specific linguistic features (Biber 1988).

In general, the stylistic differences between speech and writing can be described in terms of contrasting lexico-syntactic features: written texts typically have a higher lexical density coupled with a simpler sentence structure (Halliday 1994), features which tend to give rise to a greater economy of expression. In applying these contrasts to subtitling it is important to take account of two factors: most subtitles are a representation of spoken dialogue, thus they still need to maintain an oral flavour; secondly, their 'written features' are likely to be as much due to the need to condense utterances as to the written format of subtitles. It is also possible that the more structured syntax of written language partly compensates for the absence of phonetic and physical cues which support spoken language.

dialogue and corresponding subtitles:

nk you could, you might have learned to drive
n't believe that you would do it and take your
ve to take, you have to take your test in a gear-
Shadow like their automatic, so you couldn't

)

ake your test in a white Rolls-Royce because
ar-change car and a White Shadow like that is

)

:ontain roughly the same information. The subti-
nsequently has a higher lexical density (Halliday
tures to maintain a strong spoken orientation.
itions between spoken and written language can
e, the relatively higher lexical density of written
minalize verbal elements (e.g. *Spoken*: 'Good
Reflection is a characteristic of good writers,
nouns has been termed 'grammatical metaphor'
the actual state of events. Take for example the

following two sentences:

Spoken:	People are concerned about noise pollution, so they have been bringing private civil actions
Written:	Popular concern over noise pollution has *stimulated* private civil action.

The written version contains one clause with the verb *stimulate* representing the underlying process, i.e. the 'thesis' which is encoded as a single happening – A (concern over noise pollution) brought about B (civil action). This has been effected because the processes underlying A and B have also been nominalized. In contrast, the spoken version represents the thesis as two distinct processes linked by a causal relation: if there is concern about noise pollution civil action will occur. In this respect, the written text represents two events (one mental and one material) as one process which is neither. This type of semantic coding of two processes as if they were a single process is a common feature of writing (Halliday 1985) and illustrates the subtle changes in meaning which can arise from stylistic alterations.

In addition to linguistic considerations, there is an important related political issue regarding the form of subtitles. Many deaf people feel they should have the same information as everyone else. In a recent survey commissioned by the Independent Television Commission (ITC 1996) over half (54%) of the 458 respondents said they wanted word-for-word subtitles, while (33%) opted for summarized excerpts (13%) had no preference). When respondents were asked to consider the practical difficulties of reading word-for-word subtitles, however, the number in favour dropped by 10% resulting in a roughly even split between the two methods – word-for-word (45%) versus summarized (43%) (ITC 1996).

4.2.2 Text cohesion

The overriding demand to reduce the amount of dialogue means that many omissions have to be made on a selective basis. Although this process is often considered straightforward, it has been shown in chapter one that even slight omissions can cause a significant change in meaning.

The purpose of this section is to describe the function of cohesive elements in texts which play an important role in text comprehension. These elements are often omitted in subtitling as they are non-content bearing. However, the following sections illustrate their importance and explore the kind of linguistic issues which have to be considered when a dialogue is converted into subtitles.

Text cohesion has been defined as the grammatical and/or lexical relationships between different elements of a text (Richards et al. 1985). These relationships are supported by cohesive devices. The most comprehensive analysis of these devices has been carried out by Halliday and Hasan (1976), who identified four principal types:

*   Referential
*   Substitution and Ellipsis
*· Conjunction
*   Lexical cohesion

Each of these devices is described below.

4.2.3 Referential cohesion

As the term implies, this form of cohesive device involves referring either backwards (anaphorically) or forwards (cataphorically) to related elements in a text. Take for example the following subtitles:

> A *woman* and *her* lover went on trial for a second time today accused of plotting to murder *her* husband by faking a lawn mower accident. *Susan Whybrow* and Dennis Saunders were convicted three years ago of conspiring to murder Christopher Whybrow. But the Court of Appeal ruled they hadn't had a fair trial.
> (*News* HTV, 14.03.94).

In this example, the terms *Susan Whybrow* and *her* refer to the same individual whose identity is established in the opening sentence. The subsequent items can only be interpreted by pointing the reader back to the noun in the first sentence. Cataphoric references point the reader forwards. For example, the word *woman* anticipates a given individual. It draws us further into the text in order to identify the individual to which the reference refers. Cataphoric references are often used for dramatic effect. Other forms of referential devices include demonstrative references (e.g. 'this', 'that') or comparative references (e.g. 'greater than', 'the other' ...).

A further distinction is made between exophoric and endophoric relationships. If the interpretation of a term depends on an external referent, the relationship is said to be exophoric. Alternatively, if a term relates to an element within the same text, the relationship is described as endophoric. The distinction is particularly significant in subtitling as many textual elements have visual referents.

4.2.4 Substitution and Ellipsis

Substitution and Ellipsis are closely associated (Halliday and Hasan 1976) as they both point to a previous item in a text (Halliday 1985) either through an explicit reference (substitution) or an implied reference (ellipsis).

Take for example the following three excerpts, each containing one kind of substitution (either nominal, verbal or clausal):

Nominal: 'I've already had one *grilling* this morning. I don't need another *one* thank you.'
(*EastEnders*, BBC1, 15.03.94)

Verbal: 'You might have *learned to drive* in a white Rolls-Royce, but I don't believe that you would *do ...*'
(*Home Truths*, BBC1, 25.02.94)

Clausal: A: '*It's all pound, shillings and pence to me*'
B: 'Probably *was* the last time you had anything to do with it.'
(*Absolutely Fabulous*, BBC1, 03.03.94).

In each of the above the initial italic text has been replaced by '*one*', '*do*' and '*was*' in the subsequent sentence. These words can only be interpreted in relation to what has gone before. Ellipsis is similar except that the initial text is not substituted but merely implied by the context. For example;

A: Do us a *bacon butty* will you Michele.
B: Make it three
(*EastEnders*, BBC1, 15.03.94)

The phrase 'Make it three', like the above examples, has no complete meaning on its own without reference to previous text (i.e. '*bacon butty*'). However, unlike substitution, it makes no explicit reference to an element of the previous text (i.e. 'Make it three *of them*'). Ellipsis like substitution can occur in the same variety of forms, i.e. nominal, verbal or clausal.

4.2.5 Conjunction

Conjunctions are unlike other cohesive devices in that they are not anaphoric in nature. They do not refer back to another word or phrase used earlier in a text, rather they signal relationships between parts of a text. There are four main types of conjunctions: additive (and, or); adversative (but, however); causal (so, consequently), and temporal (then, finally) (Halliday 1985). The following dialogue contains examples of each:

We switched off the blood pressure medicine that was causing depression, *but (adversative)* it's what I call the vicious cycle syndrome, you start with drug A and *(additive) then (temporal)* they put you on drug B, *and (additive)* drug C ... and pretty soon you are taking a handful of pills, all *because (causal)* of the first drug.
(*Oprah Winfrey Show*, Channel 4, 07.03.94).

The cohesive devices themselves do not create the relationships in the text, they simply make them explicit. Often the simple juxtaposition of two clauses is enough to signal a relation-ship (e.g. She entered. She sat down). The insertion of a conjunction serves to overtly mark the relation (She entered, then she sat down).

4.2.6 Lexical cohesion

Lexical cohesion is produced when two words in a text are semantically related in some way. The two most common forms are reiteration and collocation (Halliday and Hasan 1976).

Examples of re-iteration occur in the following dialogue:

> The Lady who takes 40 *pills* (1) a day, or a week, ... um there are hypertensive *drugs* (2) *(superordinate)* that are once a day, ... instead of taking two, twice a day, or three times a day ... and then the other *drugs* (3) *(repetition)* that she has to take because of the side effects are those.
> (*Oprah Winfrey Show*, Channel 4, 07.03.94)

There are two types of reiteration which operate in the passage. The first is through the use of synonyms (i.e. 'pills' (1) and 'drugs' (2)), and the second through the use of repetition (i.e. 'drugs' (2) and 'drugs' (3)). Another common type of re-iteration involves the use of subordi-nates (e.g. *drugs* ÷ paracetamol) and general references (e.g. drugs ÷ those *things*).

Collocation is harder to identify as it includes all those items in a text which regularly oc-cur together, including prepositions, verbs, nouns, etc. For example, the word 'high' collocates with 'probability', but not with 'chance' ('high probability' rather than 'high chance') (Richards 1985).

Part of the difficulty in identifying collocating words is that the list appears infinitely extend-able. Lexical relationships not only vary according to text type but also with context. Two words or phrases related in one text may not be related in another. Familiarity with the content is also thought to play a greater role in perceiving these types of cohesive ties. However, it has been argued that lexical cohesion is the single most important form of cohesion, accounting for something like 40% of cohesive ties in texts (Hoey 1991).

4.2.7 Text cohesion and subtitles

Cohesive devices play an important role in making relationships between entities and events explicit. In the process of condensing dialogue to subtitle text there is therefore an issue whether these elements should be omitted. Although the intention might be to simplify a text, omission of cohesive devices can lead to a text becoming more difficult to process and result in a loss of meaning. Processing difficulties may also be compounded by the fact that subtitles are a transi-tory written form, often with exophoric references to the screen image, forcing a viewer to alternate between linguistic and visual sources.

Taking the example subtitle cited above, it is possible to see how the meaning of the text has been subtly altered through the removal of a few cohesive elements:

Subtitle: It's a vicious cycle. You start with drug A, then drug B, then soon you are taking a handful of drugs.

Speech: It's what I call the vicious cycle syndrome. You start with drug A and then they put you on drug B, and drug C, and pretty soon you are taking a handful of pills, *all because* of the first drug.
(*Oprah Winfrey Show*, Channel 4, 07.03.94).

Through the removal of the reiterative subordinate synonym *pills* and the final phrase beginning *all because* the subtitled text indicates a different causual relationship to the original dialogue. Hence a viewer could quite reasonably assume that the speaker was talking about accumulative drug taking rather than the self-perpetuating nature of certain medical pills.

The importance of cohesive devices has been well established (Davison 1988, Ewoldt 1984) partly through examining the various effects that result from their omission. The following example is taken from a story that has been simplified for deaf people (Ewoldt 1984). The original story, 'To Build a Fire' (London 1968) is about a character with no personality, thoughts, or feelings, who goes outside in cold weather in the Yukon and freezes to death. In the rewritten version certain cohesive devices are omitted, which not only appears to affect the story's literary quality but also tends to muddy the plot, illustrating the effect of omitting temporal conjunctions.

Rewritten: The dog sat and watched him.
             The dog sat in the snow.
             It whined. The man remained silent. It crept close to the man and caught the scent of death.

Original: *And all the while* the dog sat and watched him.
             and all the while the dog sat in the snow.
             It whined softly. But the man remained silent. *Later*, the dog whined loudly. *And still later* it crept close to the man and caught the scent of death.

Although the text is comprehensible, it trivializes the dog's suffering and removes all poignancy from the story.

Similar effects result from the omission of repetitious elements. In the following example, repetition is used to generate an ominous mood in a passage about a man exposed to the cold.

Rewritten: There was no mistake about it, it was cold.

Original: Once in a while the thought reiterated itself that it was very *cold* and that he had never experienced such *cold*. It certainly was *cold*.

Such cohesive devices can contribute to the readability of a text as well as performing a rhetorical function. This effect is thought to derive from the fact that recurring structures or vocabulary are more predictable and, therefore, easier to read (Ewoldt 1984).

4.3   Film features

As stated in the introduction, subtitles must integrate with the existing material and semiotic structure of a film. In order to properly understand this process, it is necessary to have a basic appreciation of the properties of the film medium. While film cannot be said to be as rule governed as language, some of its systematic features and conventions have been described (Turner 1994). Many of these conventions are not immediately apparent to a viewer but in fact contribute to the overall meaning of a film. In addition, certain conventions have a direct effect on the form of subtitles.

A good example of the interaction between subtitles and film can be seen in the case of shot-reverse-shot sequencing, used to represent the interpersonal dynamics of conversation (c.f.

figure 24). The camera frames each speaker in turn, positioning them on opposite sides (one to the right and the other to the left) of the frame. Besides extending the boundaries of the frame to include both parties, this has the effect of indicating that the people are communicating with each other (similar in many ways to sign language depiction of a conversation).

With oral dialogue, a viewer is able to identify who is speaking at any particular time by following the tone of voice. With subtitles, however, this kind of sequencing can quickly lead to confusion, as without voice monitoring the only possible form of indication is strict speaker-comment coordination. In other words, the eye has to scan image and subtitle in succession in order to identify a speaker. This is particularly the case when dialogue becomes rapid or when the camera jumps to capture the facial reaction of an interlocutor. The resulting confusion is thought not only to disrupt the reading of a current subtitle but also of subsequent subtitles (Baker 1982, de Linde 1995).

The following sections focus on two important aspects of film 'language', camera manipulation and editing, in order to illustrate the basic features of the medium. When considering these features, it is important to remember that the visual narrative on screen maybe as important to a deaf viewer as the textual narrative in subtitles.

4.3.1 *Camera manipulation*

Camera manipulation is probably the most complex area of film production. Choice of camera angle, field depth, movement and framing all contribute semiotically to a film or television programme. It is therefore important to understand the parameters which govern camera manipulation in order to appreciate the complexity of information in the screen image.

Camera position is perhaps the most obvious variable in television and film production. Conventional Camera positions range from panoramic overheads or 'crane shots' to intimate focusing of a subject angled squarely or obliquely. The camera can rotate along either the vertical axis (panning), the horizontal axis (tilting), or the transverse axis (rolling), each conveying a particular meaning or impression.

Panning a camera along the horizontal axis imitates the movement of a spectator surveying the scene around them. Such movements can be used to associate with the perspective of a character. Rolling the camera gives the illusion of the world, either actually or metaphorically, being tipped on its side. This technique is also used to give a subjective impression of events, for example to indicate that a character is falling, drugged or sick (Turner 1994).

Tracking or dollying (forward or lateral movement of the camera apparatus) is often used to cover action sequences and, again, to identify with a character's experience. An example of how this shot can also affect subtitles occurred in an episode of *How Do They Do That?* (BBC1), examining the movements of acrobats in an advert for Halifax Building Society (c.f. Figure 25).

In this example, the visual sequence is effective when accompanied by dialogue but not when accompanied by subtitles. The discourse in such sequences often simply serves to elucidate the action, reinforcing immediately what is visible on screen. This does not pose a problem when both mediums can be processed simultaneously as sound and image. However, when both mediums are competing for the same visual channel, as with text and image, they can only be processed in succession. This often results in a sort of 'cubist' reading of the sequence, where image and text no longer complement each other but appear juxtaposed.

Camera height and distance from a subject can also affect the meaning of a shot. For example, a narrative closure is often indicated by slowly pulling the camera away so that subjects disappear into their surroundings. This either enhances the ambiguity of an emotional response or invites viewers to project their own emotions onto the scene.

The effect of close-up shots in face-to-face interaction is widely acknowledged. Politicians have for a long time been aware of the importance of gazing straight into the camera while reading from a script. Both President Reagan and Margaret Thatcher were well known for insisting on a 'Head-up Display Unit' – a kind of autocue known to politicians as the 'sincerity machine' (Cockerell 1988:276). Patterns of eye-contact often reflect the status and authority of participants:

> If we switch on our sets and see someone addressing us directly, we know he is a narrator or presenter. If his gaze is directed slightly off-camera, we know he is an interviewee, a talking head. If he is turned away from us by an angle of more than about 15 degrees he is part of an action sequence. It is clear that there is a hierarchy of authority implicit in this code. The talking head is permitted to gaze into the sacred sector only through the priest-like intercession of the interviewer: and, if he should speak directly to the camera, he will create an impression of insolence.
> (Vaughan 1976:16, cited by Masterman 1980:50)

The proximity convention of natural conversation is also exploited in television news. Physical distance is commonly associated with social distance. Ordinary people, particularly when distressed, may be shown in close-up in a way which evokes intimacy but also positions them as less powerful. Politicians and other important figures are, in contrast, framed at a more respectable distance, usually within the range of what could be described as formal to casual (Graddol 1994).

4.3.2 Editing

The most important aspect of editing is the construction of relationships between individual shots. Editing usually involves creating an impression of continuity in time and space. Exceptionally, film is edited to enhance action sequences or shots of highly dramatic content (i.e. 'montage'), but in general the craft of the editor 'is to remain invisible and knit the shots together according to realist aesthetics' (Turner 1994).

There are a multitude of editing techniques used to guide the viewer between shots (fade-out, dissolve, wipe-out, etc.). The most basic method is the simple 'cut'. However, a straightforward 'cut' can appear sudden and disorientating and so is usually reserved for dramatic sequences involving surprise, horror or disruption. A cut is also acceptable when a shot change follows the logical structure of a narrative. In other cases, complementary devices can be used to smooth a transition, for example overlapping sound from one shot to the next. The timing of cuts can also be used to either intensify or control the energy of a scene, as in action sequences where rapid cuts can heighten the sense of drama and complexity (Turner 1994).

Other editorial conventions include shot-reverse-shot sequencing, (described earlier, c.f. Figure 24), the use of short establishing shots to place a narrative in a new location, and the strict observation of an imaginary line across a film set over which the camera never crosses so that the viewer is given a consistent representation of the spatial relations between actors and their surroundings (c.f. 'the 180° rule', Turner 1994).

The speed, pace and rhythm of editing is also important. Documentary film contains fewer edits than narrative film, a feature which is often imitated in social-realist productions. Many feature films maintain an identifiable rhythm throughout, against which the editing in individual sequences can be measured to alter dramatic intensity (Turner 1994).

4.3.3 Film features and subtitles

The previous section has provided an introduction to some of the main features of film production, describing the standard techniques employed in camera manipulation and editing. These features are fundamental to the material structure of films and form part of their semiotics.

In examining the relationship between these features and subtitles, it is essential to bear in mind that films and television programmes are designed on the basis of oral dialogue within an audio soundtrack. When spoken discourse is replaced by written discourse the structure of the medium is altered, changing the balance between oral and visual channels. Screen images and linguistic discourse can no longer be processed simultaneously, and this affects the way a film is received.

The possible disruption in meaning, resulting from a shift in communication channels from oral and visual to solely visual, has been illustrated above with reference to a Halifax Building Society advert analyzed in the programme *How Do They Do That?* (BBC1, c.f. Figure 25). Here the meaning of the original dialogue, complementing the screen action, was lost when transformed into written subtitles.

In general, the most direct effect of film structure on subtitles is through the varied and extensive use of shot changes. A number of studies have shown that shot changes can cause major disruption to reading (Baker 1982, de Linde 1995). One study in particular identified preferential editing techniques (d'Ydewalle and Vanderbeeken 1996). When presented with two different editing methods – one stressing the importance of perceptual continuity between successive shots, the other stressing the importance of narrative continuity – results showed support for the former method (d'Ydewalle 1996). These findings reinforce the significance of film language as a medium of communication. In fact research into news bulletins (Graddol 1994) has shown that different roles exist for each medium: 'the verbal channel speaks of causes whilst the visual tells of effects' (Graddol 1994).

4.4   Summary

This chapter has analyzed the text and film elements of subtitling. Each element has been examined individually as well as the effect of their integration in subtitled television. In addition to the specific issues highlighted here, it would be useful to conduct further research on the linguistic characteristics of subtitles, and how the presence or absence of these characteristics affects the viewing process (c.f. chapters seven and eight). It would also be valuable to explore further elements of film 'language' which have an influence on subtitling.

Chapter Five: Studying the Effect of Subtitles

5.1   Introduction

As noted in the initial chapter, inter- and intralingual subtitling have tended to be studied from different perspectives. Interlingual subtitling is typically viewed as a form of translation while intralingual subtitling has largely been seen as an assistive aid for deaf people, based on editing (Norwood 1988, Thorn 1990). Consequently, the questions asked of each form have differed. Studies of interlingual subtitling have largely dealt with translation issues within a broad linguistic/cultural framework; studies of intralingual subtitling, on the other hand, have largely focused on the communicative effectiveness of the medium for deaf and hard-of-hearing viewers.

In line with the holistic approach of this study, previous chapters have described some of the linguistic aspects of both types of subtitling while this chapter now examines the main studies that have sought to evaluate the efficacy of the medium. These studies have been particularly important in providing insights about how subtitles are received in practice. They also form a background to the experimental research in the study described in the following chapters.

Studies of the effectiveness of subtitles tend to follow three broad approaches, differing in the degree to which experimental variables are controlled. The first approach involves eliciting viewers' responses to questions about their experience of subtitled television. The second approach attempts to go further in looking at viewers' responses to different sets of pre-categorized subtitles. The third approach applies control to both medium and viewer in order to gain precise behavioural information about how particular subtitle characteristics are received.

The three approaches are described in detail below with reference to the major studies using each method:

- Survey method
- Semi-controlled experiment method
- Controlled experiment method

5.2   Survey method

As outlined above, the survey method is used to collect general information about viewers' reactions to subtitled television; in particular, the differences of opinion held within a population on a variety of issues. It is not designed to provide an explanation of viewers' opinions or to analyze viewing behaviour.

One of the largest studies of this kind was jointly conducted by the IBA and BBC in 1988 (Gunter 1988). The aim was to design two surveys to investigate on a national scale public opinion towards the use of sign language inserts and subtitles for the deaf and hard-of-hearing (surveys were addressed to both deaf and hearing viewers). Questions were put to a national television viewing panel about their awareness and experience of these aids, in particular, how favourable they were towards the use of such aids in different kinds of programmes (Gunter 1988).

The surveys were conducted with BARB's Television Opinion Panel, comprising 3,550 individuals, who received a booklet each week containing a 'viewing diary' and supplementary questions on particular programmes and wider broadcasting-related issues. One survey canvassed opinion on television subtitles while the other focused on the use of sign language inserts (Gunter 1988).

There were 3,297 'usable returns' from the survey on subtitles and 3,550 returns from the survey on sign language inserts. Not surprisingly, viewers with hearing problems tended to be more favourable to signing and subtitling for a larger number of programmes. General opinions about signing and subtitles were mixed. Although viewers agreed on the use of these aids for hearing impaired people in principle, there was some concern for their own enjoyment of programmes. Many viewers felt that signing and subtitling in their favourite programmes might take a bit of getting used to (Gunter 1988; c.f. Norwood study, Chapter one).

A more recent study, using a similar method, focused on the opinions of deaf and hard-of-hearing viewers (Kyle 1993). Views were elicited on three key aspects of television subtitling: programme preferences, viewing strategies, and subtitle characteristics. The study was structured around two questionnaires: a short postal questionnaire and an extended questionnaire followed up by interviews. A total of 2,500 deaf and hard-of-hearing viewers participated in the study. A small group of them were also invited to keep diaries on their viewing over a week.

The questions on programme preferences revealed differences amongst the participants based on age and type of hearing loss. In general, younger viewers preferred popular programmes; older viewers preferred serious programmes; hard-of-hearing viewers preferred 'highbrow and serious', and deaf viewers preferred films and comedy.

The questions on viewing strategy again revealed differences between deaf and hard-of-hearing viewers. If there were no subtitles, deaf viewers were more likely to switch off or attempt to guess at the dialogue, while hard-of-hearing viewers were more likely to try to listen with their hearing aids.

The third set of questions on subtitle characteristics revealed more specific information: lagging (the delay between speech and subtitle) mainly affected drama programmes; colour changes had little effect on information retention; add-on lines were seldom detected by viewers, and comprehension did not seem to be affected by varying the format of subtitles – although it did affect enjoyment (Kyle 1991).

Studies based on the survey method have not always involved a large number of participants. A study by Woll (1991) explored the preferences of 57 deaf and hard-of-hearing people about programmes adapted for deaf viewers. Participants were asked several questions about the mix of signing and subtitling. Again, questions were divided between viewers' strategies and preferences.

Results showed that most viewers used a combination of methods to access programme information. The most common approach (reported by 46% of viewers) was to use every resource available (deaf translators, hearing interpreters, subtitles) except lip reading. However, the preferred mode of communication (58%) was a combination of signing and subtitling (Woll 1991).

A common characteristic of the survey method is the use of questionnaires to obtain information from viewers. This technique is useful in examining general opinions on a wide range of issues. However, more controlled conditions are necessary to obtain specific information on viewers' reactions to different subtitle features.

5.3   Semi-controlled experiment method

The semi-controlled experiment method has been used to elicit specific information about the effect of particular subtitle features. It goes further than the survey method in keeping all programme variables constant, except the one being examined. A study based on this method was conducted by Gregory (1996), who examined children's reactions to different styles of subtitling. The study focused on two medium variables: subtitle complexity and programme type, categorizing children's responses according to age.

Each participant (n=77) watched two short clips from two different types of programme, subtitled at three levels of complexity. After each clip, children were asked to recount what they had watched to either a hearing researcher or a researcher fluent in British Sign Language (BSL). The viewing sessions and subsequent interviews lasted approximately thirty minutes.

The results of the study confirmed that the participants who retained most information were those who made greatest use of the subtitles. The amount of correct information retained from the subtitles was also in direct relation to the age of participants. For all programme types and over all age groups, the simplified subtitles appeared to provide participants with the greatest amount of information, as opposed to the 'basic' or 'complex' subtitles (Gregory 1996).

Another study using this method focused on the transmission of non-speech information or 'NSI' (e.g. sound effects, music, manner of speaking, audience reaction, etc.) (TAP 1993). Subtitles can include various representations of NSI, such as italics, text placement, upper/lower case lettering, symbols '<<', etc. One aim of the study was to explore the effectiveness of a variety of methods of representing non-speech information. Nineteen different representations of NSI were examined in the study. Each feature of NSI was represented in two or three alternative ways. Viewers (106 deaf and 83 hard-of-hearing) were asked to state a preference for either alternative.

Results showed that explicit speaker identification (by name) was the preferred means of indicating a particular speaker. Quotation marks followed by italics were less favoured but considered acceptable. Colour and flashing text were thought unacceptable.

Both the above studies used controlled experimental conditions to record information about viewers' reactions to different subtitle features. By controlling variables and limiting viewers' responses, more specific information can be gained by experiments based on this method than by those based on the survey method.

5.4   Controlled experiment method

The controlled experiment method has more in common with the semi-controlled experiment method than with the survey method in that it is used to analyze the effects of particular medium variables on viewing characteristics. However, rather than eliciting viewers' reactions, experiments following this method are designed to record actual motor behaviour. By analyzing optic pauses and regressions, and monitoring the pace of reading, detailed information can be obtained about the viewing process. This can be done relatively unobtrusively with modern eye-movement monitors.

A number of studies have been conducted using this technique, both on inter- and intralingual subtitles. Many of these have been carried out at the University of Leuven, addressing a variety of issues: the relationship between subtitle comprehension and familiarity with the medium (d'Ydewalle et al. 1988); parafoveal and peripheral processing of subtitles (Gielen and d'Ydewalle 1992); differences in attention shift between children and adults (d'Ydewalle and Van Rensbergen 1989), and information recall (Gielen and d'Ydewalle 1992). Similar studies examining medium variables have analyzed the effect of subtitle presentation times (d'Ydewalle et al. 1987) and access to sound (ibid).

Comparatively fewer studies have focused on subtitling for deaf people. A research project conducted at Leuven (Verfaillie and d'Ydewalle 1987) analyzed modality preferences in deaf people educated within the oral tradition. Three different linguistic sources of information were presented: subtitles, sign language, and lip-reading. All subjects were shown programmes in four different modes:

- Speaker, sign interpreter and subtitles simultaneously
- Subtitles and sign interpreter
- Subtitles and speaker
- Speaker and sign interpreter.

The study revealed a strong preference for subtitles. When enough time remained after reading the subtitles, participants focused on other areas of the screen. When no subtitles were shown, participants showed a preference for sign language, although they were not able to fully comprehend the meaning of a programme. Participants showed better comprehension with subtitles than without, and the presence of sign interpretation appeared to have an adverse effect on programme comprehension (Verfaillie and d'Ydewalle 1987).

The results of this study are partly corroborated by a study described earlier which surveyed viewers' opinions on different forms of language transfer (Woll 1991). Woll's study also showed a preference for subtitles.

The only eye-movement research examining deaf peoples' viewing behaviour has been conducted at the University of Southampton (Baker 1982). The eye-movement patterns of two 'post-lingually' deaf adults were analyzed in a pilot study. Owing to difficulties in obtaining accurate eye-movement recordings, and the fact that 'no specific hypotheses had been set prior to the viewing session', the resulting data was primarily used for hypothesis generation (ibid).

Despite these difficulties, the study produced some interesting findings. Reading rates and the time taken to fixate on a subtitle appeared to be influenced by a number of factors: the presence or absence of audible/ visible speech cues and various types of 'false alarms' (e.g. the expectation of a new subtitle) were shown to have disruptive effects on the reading of the current subtitle and also subsequent subtitles. Regressive eye-movements indicated specific syntactic and vocabulary difficulties and suggested that a working criterion for maximum on-screen time (as well as minimum on-screen time) could be set (ibid). Baker was cautious about the results of the study which were presented as a basis for further research.

As shown by the above studies, eye-movement experiments are able to provide very precise quantitative information on how people watch subtitled television, leading to judgements about the effectiveness of particular features. However, taken on their own, these measurements can be ambiguous. For example, a low number of eye fixations could either indicate an exceptionally able reader or a viewer who is hardly reading at all. Consequently, the data produced from eye-movement experiments has to be supported by tests gauging viewers' comprehension and an examination of both visual and linguistic material.

5.5   Summary

This chapter has explored a number of studies that have investigated viewers' reactions on subtitling and/or attempted to examine the effectiveness of subtitles. The results of these studies give important insights into viewers' preferences and the comparative effects of alternative subtitle formats.

Three broad research methods have been described: the survey method, the semi-controlled experiment method, and the controlled experiment method. Each approach is suitable for eliciting certain types of information, ranging from viewers' opinions to eye-movement behaviour. The different methods also complement each other in producing a broad, detailed picture of how subtitles are processed and received.

Chapter Six: Subtitling for Adults

6.1   Introduction

The previous chapter reviewed a number of research studies dealing with the effect and effectiveness of subtitles. The aim of this chapter, and chapter seven is to set this research in the context of actual subtitled programmes on British television.

As noted in chapter two, relatively little is known about the typical characteristics of subtitles broadcast for deaf and hard-of-hearing people. For example, there is no accurate information on standard display times, how these times differ according to programme type, the synchronization of speech and subtitles or the integration of subtitles and image. This information is important on two accounts: to gauge the results of previous research and to identify characteristic features of broadcast subtitles in order to inform future studies on viewing behaviour.

Subtitled television comprises three main components: image, subtitles and spoken dialogue. The integration of these components, combined with viewers' reading capacities, determines the basic characteristics of the medium. Subtitles have to synchronize with both speech and image, present an accurate interpretation of a dialogue and remain on screen long enough for them to be read by viewers.

In order to assess these basic requirements, a cross-section of British subtitled television was recorded and analyzed to provide base-line measures of current output for adults and children. This chapter presents the characteristics of subtitled television for adults, while the following chapter presents similar information about subtitled television for children.

The following variables were recorded:

- Synchronicity between subtitle and dialogue (including speech rates, subtitle rates, lead and lag times)
- Synchronicity between image and subtitle (i.e. shot changes)
- Extent of editing

The 'readability' of each programme script was also measured by a standard index. However, these results were later felt not to be informative and were therefore not used in the analysis (c.f. Appendix One).

6.2   Subtitle samples

Subtitle samples were drawn from daily recordings of six hours of television over approximately one month (21 February 1994 to 18 March 1994, excluding weekends) between 17:30hrs and 23:30hrs. A different channel was recorded each day in order to produce a representative set of statistics (Table 4).

The number of subtitled programmes varied across the four channels. Figure 5 displays the proportion of programmes subtitled on each: BBC1, BBC2, HTV, and CH4. These figures are based solely on the sampling scheme described in table 4.

Over half of all programme output was subtitled at this peak time. Seventy-six per cent of all output on Channel 4 was subtitled (excluding advertisements), compared with 70% of programmes on BBC1, 56% on HTV, and 53% on BBC2.

	Week 1	Week 2	Week 3	Week 4
Monday	BBC1	BBC2	CH4	HTV
Tuesday	BBC2	CH4	HTV	BBC1
Wednesday	CH4	HTV	BBC1	BBC2
Thursday	HTV	BBC1	BBC2	CH4
Friday	BBC1	BBC2	CH4	HTV

Table 4: Pattern of Television Recordings

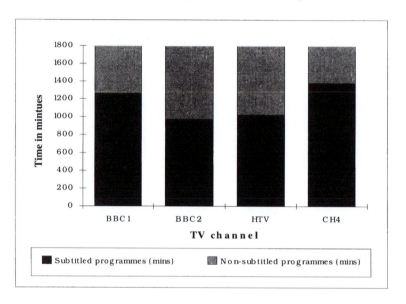

Figure 5: Proportion of Subtitled and Non-subtitled Programmes (n = 120 hours)

6.3   Selection and analysis procedure

For sampling purposes all programmes were classified according to programme type.

The categories were based partly on conventional programme types (as used by the ITC and BBC) such as news and drama serials, and also on discourse style, e.g. full-face news reader or voice-over. The number of categories was restricted to ten. On the whole, programmes corresponded neatly to the type categories with only a few exceptions. *Top of the Pops*, for example, might have been more appropriate for a separate 'music' category. However, as the discourse style approximates to that associated with 'magazine' programmes, it was classified under 'magazine'. None of the categories are exclusive: a drama serial may contain incidents of narration more commonly found in documentaries, and likewise documentaries may include episodes of interactive dialogue more characteristic of drama serials.

Figure 6 shows the proportion of programmes subtitled according to programme type (on all four channels). The most frequently subtitled programme types were National News (100%), Drama Serials (89%) and Film (66%). Regional News, Sports, and Cartoons were not subtitled (with the exception of some children's Cartoons (see chapter seven). Dialogue in most 'adult' cartoons rarely contains essential linguistic information; there are often simply sound sequences identified with a particular character or mood. As many of these sounds do not affect understanding, there is no imperative to produce accompanying subtitles. In fact, transcribing incidental sounds may cause confusion (Baker 1982). Likewise, sports commentaries are rarely subtitled as their function is to reinforce the action on screen. The addition of subtitles would divert viewers' attention away from the image and therefore lessen their appreciation (Baker 1982).

Programme Type	Example Programme
Cartoon (CART)	e.g. *Peter Pan*
Comedy (CO)	e.g. *Absolutely Fabulous*
Documentary (DOC)	e.g. *Omnibus*
Drama Serial (DS)	e.g. *Coronation Street*
Film (FI)	e.g. *Dead Calm*
Game/Chat Show (G/CH)	e.g. *The Oprah Winfrey Show*
Magazine (MAG)	e.g. *Watchdog*
National News (N)	e.g. *News, Newsnight*
Regional News (RN)	e.g. *HTV News*
Sport (SP)	e.g. *Sportsnight*

Table 5: Examples of Programme Types

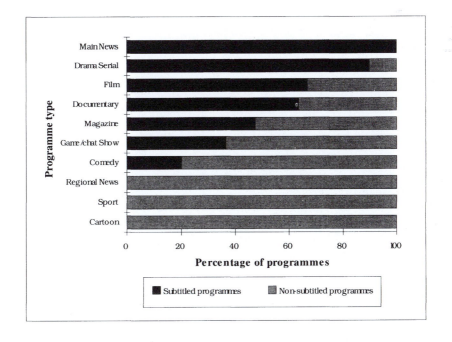

Figure 6: Percentage of Programme Types (n = 218 programmes)

Programme	First sample	Second sample	Number of subtitles
Comedy	Absolutely Fabulous (BBC1)	Absolutely Fabulous (BBC1)	30+31 = 61
Documentary	Horizon (BBC2)	In Search of Our Ancestors (BBC2)	22+17 = 39
Drama Serial	EastEnders (BBC1)	Brookside (CH4)	17+22 = 39
Film	Dead Calm (BBC1)	All Things Bright and Beautiful (BBC2)	25+23 = 48
Chat Show	Oprah Winfrey Show (CH4)	Home Truths (BBC1)	23+21 = 44
Magazine	How Do They Do That? (BBC1)	How Do They Do That? (BBC1)	18+13 = 31
National News	(Sample not included)	(Sample not included)	TOTAL = 262
Regional News	(No subtitles available)	(No subtitles available)	
Cartoon	(No subtitles available)	(No subtitles available)	
Sport	(No subtitles available)	(No subtitles available)	

Table 6: Sample Programmes Subtitled for Adults

The samples chosen for analysis consisted of two minutes of subtitled television drawn randomly from each of the programme types (total number of samples = 262). The programmes selected are outlined in Table 6 (National News was not analyzed in the study as the process of 'quasi-live' subtitling differs markedly from other programme types):

Figure 7: Sample Subtitle

Measurements of speech, subtitle and image were recorded for each sample as illustrated in Figure 7 and Table 8 Subtitle times are accurate to 0.04 of a second and speech times to 0.5 of a second. The relative inaccuracy of speech times was due to the difficulty in anticipating the onset and offset of non-visual information. Speech times include pauses between words and phrases. Shot changes occurring during a subtitle were briefly described, with emphasis placed on the positions of speaker and hearer. The number of subtitles per two-minute sample varied between 13 (magazine) and 31 (comedy).

Table 7 displays the key information from the sample television shot shown in Figure 7. The information includes:

- Onset and offset times of speech (0.92 and 4.72 seconds respectively).
- Appearance and disappearance time of subtitle (0.00 and 5.56 seconds respectively).
- Description of shots over-running subtitles.

All measurements were taken from the start of the subtitle. Thus the on-set time of speech is recorded as 0.92 as it began 0.92 seconds after the start of the subtitle. Speech occasionally begins before a subtitle in which case the time difference was marked as negative.
Subtitles often overlap with shots relating to previous and subsequent subtitles. For instance, in the above example the first shot is carried over from the previous subtitle, and the last shot overlaps with the following subtitle. Research has suggested that if shot changes occur during a subtitle, this can lead to re-reading (Baker 1982).

From the resulting data, three pieces of information were established:

- Synchronicity between subtitle and sound

- Synchronicity between image and subtitle
- Extent of editing

Measurements to calculate the degree of synchronicity between subtitle and sound included: duration of speech; duration of subtitle; 'on-set' and 'off-set' times of subtitles relative to speech ... In Table 7 speech duration is 6.8 seconds; subtitle time is 5.56 seconds; 'lead-in' time is 0.92 seconds; and 'off-set' time is 0.84 seconds.

The degree of synchronicity between images and subtitles was based on the number of camera shots per subtitle. In the above example (Table 7) there are two shot changes. The first shot change occurs 2.36 seconds after the appearance of the subtitle – focus shifts away from the speaker and on to the listeners, who are positioned in the foreground. The next change occurs 8.16 seconds later with a return to the original shot as shown in Figure 7. The speaker is in the foreground and the two listeners are in the background. The source of sound is 'on screen' in the sense that the speaker is visible.

The degree of editing was calculated on the basis of the difference in the number of words between a speech section and a corresponding subtitle.

Name of programme: *Absolutely Fabulous* (Comedy)			
Time in seconds	0.92 seconds		4.72 seconds
Speech	At least in my day darling, people used to go to		
	university just to close 'em down!		
Time in seconds	0.0 seconds		5.56 seconds
Subtitle	At least in my day, people went to		
	university just to close 'em down!		
Time in seconds		2.36seconds	10.52 seconds
Image	Three women	Three women	Three women
	in kitchen.Sp1.	in kitchen.Listeners	in kitchen. Sp1.
	in foreground	in foreground	in foreground

Table 7: Data Record of a Sample Subtitle

6.4   Results: characteristics of subtitles broadcast for adults

The data was analyzed to provide a comparative view of subtitle characteristics according to programme type.

6.4.1 *Synchronicity between subtitle and sound*

The speech rate is the rate at which information is presented through a soundtrack. In a previous study on programme classification, Baker and Lambourne (1984) found that 'full face' news broadcasts and live chat-shows have a higher spoken information rate than narrative-style voice-overs. Figure 8 shows the average speech rate by programme type according to the samples selected.

Speech rates were measured by taking the mean rate at which information relating to one subtitle was presented on the soundtrack (i.e. number of words ÷ time of utterance). The rate excludes pauses between utterances, thereby relating purely to textual content.

The results in Figure 8 are consistent with Baker and Lambourne (1984). Game shows, chat shows and drama serials have a higher spoken information rate (approximately 230 words per minute) than narrative-style voice-over programmes such as documentaries (195 wpm). Comedy appears to fall between both styles of programme with an average speech rate of 208 words per minute. The comedy samples had similar characteristics to the samples taken from drama serials but due to the specific conditions of comedy (rapid dialogues, quick repartee, etc.) it is not surprising that speech rates were slightly faster.

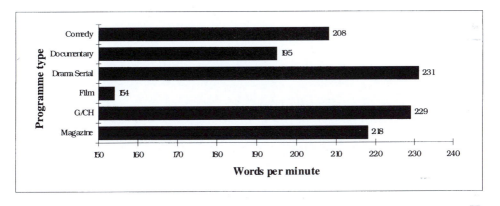

Figure 8: Speech Rates

Film had an unusually low speech rate. This was due to the particular nature of the film samples. Each sample contained a large proportion of non-speech sound such as animal noises, background music, machine bleeps and so on. These were recorded as one word utterances and consequently gave a skewed impression of the speech rate.

Subtitle presentation rate (words per minute) is a measure of how quickly a subtitle appears and disappears from screen. It is often considered synonymous with reading rate, as it determines the time a viewer has to access the written text. Suggested subtitle presentation rates vary from company to company but in general they lie between 110 and 140 words per minute (ITC 1993, BBC 1994).

Subtitle rates were measured as the number of words in a subtitle divided by presentation time. This method of analyzing subtitle rates is more appropriate than measuring the total number of subtitles per minute of film, as it excludes the time when no verbal information (oral or written) is transmitted.

The results in Figure 9 support the display times proposed by the main broadcasting companies. The more interactive style programmes – game shows, chat shows, and drama serials – had slightly higher subtitle rates (approximately 133 wpm) than the narrative based programmes: documentaries and magazines (approximately 125 wpm). Film had an unusually low subtitle rate for reasons mentioned above regarding speech rates.

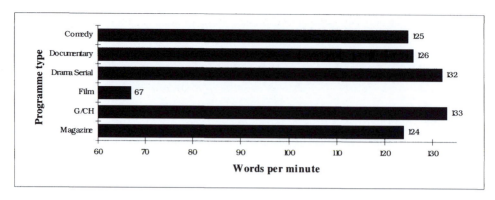

Figure 9: Subtitle Presentation Rates

Figure 10 shows that out of a sample of 262 subtitles and their corresponding speech segments the average subtitle display time was 43% less than speech time. Excluding Film (56%), percentage differences ranged from 38% for documentaries to 43% for magazines. Word omissions are discussed later under *Editing*.

A number of subtitling companies have specified minimum requirements for synchronization between subtitles and sound.

> The subtitles should match the pace of speaking as closely as possible. Ideally, when the speaker is in shot, your subtitles should not anticipate speech by more than 1.5 seconds or hang up on the screen for more than 1.5 seconds after speech has stopped. The subtitle should not be on the screen after the speaker has disappeared (BBC 1994:11).

Subtitles must not only keep in time with the beginning and end of utterances but also with the natural flow of speech. One of the primary considerations of television subtitling is to reduce the frustration felt by deaf viewers when faced with silent moving mouths. Therefore, all obvious sounds should have some form of subtitle accompaniment. It is also considered that subtitles should coincide with the beginning and end of a corresponding speech segment, since subtitles remaining too long on screen are likely to be re-read, causing an unnecessary 'false alarm' (ITC 1993).

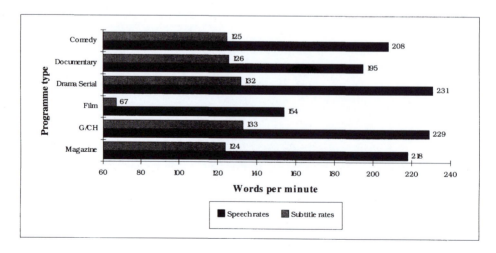

Figure 10: Speech and Subtitle Presentation Rates

Figures 11 and 12 show the on-set and off-set times of subtitles and speech. All times fall within the BBC's 1.5 second guideline. Due to the difficulty in determining the start and end of speech segments, figures are only accurate to 0.5 of a second. Thus all measures must be taken as estimates.

'Lead' time refers to the time between the on-set of a subtitle and the start of speech. 'Lag' time refers to the time between the end of speech and the off-set of a subtitle. In Figure 11, the horizontal line positioned at '0' seconds denotes the start of speech. Measurements preceding the speech line (lead times) denote subtitles starting before speech, and measurements after the speech line (lag times) denote subtitles following the onset of speech.

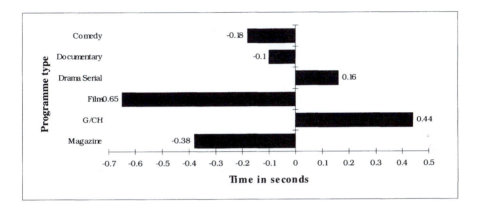

Figure 11: Mean On-set Time of Subtitles by Programme Type

In most cases, subtitles preceded the onset of speech. The exceptions were drama serials, game and chat shows. The average subtitle delay in drama serials was slight and may have been partially due to difficulties in fixing speech times. Game and chat shows however showed greater delay times. Most chat shows, and perhaps to a lesser extent game shows, have a high proportion of fast interactive dialogue. Consequently, subtitles have to be both paced with quick exchanges of speech and synchronized with accompanying shot changes. This dual requirement often makes it difficult to synchronise the onset of subtitles with speech.

Figure 12 shows the off-set times of subtitles, i.e. the time between the end of speech and the disappearance of a corresponding subtitle. Again the horizontal line at '0' seconds denotes the end of speech.

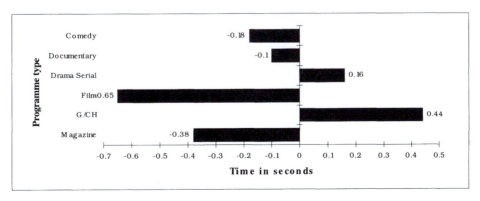

Figure 12: Mean Off-set Time of Subtitles by Programme Type

In line with broadcasting standards, all subtitles remained on screen for a long enough period after the end of associated speech. It is interesting to note that the delay time recorded for documentaries was slightly longer. Most documentaries contain a relatively high proportion of voice-over commentary. This means that subtitles are not tied to speakers' lips and facial movements and can therefore remain on screen longer without causing frustration to the viewer.

6.4.2 Synchronicity between subtitle and image

Subtitles have to synchronize with both speech and the moving image. Those which over-run shot changes can cause considerable perceptual confusion (ITC 1992). Research into eye-movement has revealed that when a shot change occurs in the middle of a subtitle, viewers return to the beginning of a partially read subtitle and start re-reading (Baker 1982). Despite efforts to break up sentences so that they fall on either side of shot changes, almost all subtitles are interrupted by a shot change. Figure 13 shows the mean number of camera shots per subtitle.

All programmes sampled had an average of more than one shot change per subtitle. Drama serials and Magazine programmes had a slightly higher proportion than others. In one instance, a subtitle was interrupted by nine separate shot changes (c.f. Figure 25). This occurred in a Magazine sample where the off-screen commentary described the actions of an acrobat moving in slow motion (see Table 8).

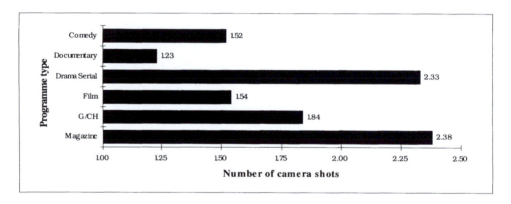

Figure 13: Mean Number of Camera Shots per Subtitle

A distinction should be made between shot changes occurring during a scene and shot changes separating major scenes. The latter can cause further confusion as a speaker's last utterance is instantly followed by a shot change, leaving the comment hanging over the next scene. A classic example of this occurred in news footage about the place where a royal couple were to spend their honeymoon. The first intended shot was of a royal palace but a subsequent overlapping shot showed a four poster bed.

6.4.3 Extent of editing

As described in the initial chapter, subtitling is constrained by spatial and temporal factors (screen size and film structure) and the reading capacities of viewers. These constraints necessitate a certain degree of editing.

A number of studies have dealt with the underlying principles of editing in interlingual subtitling, through examining the linguistic elements which are retained and omitted (de Linde 1995, Gottlieb 1992, Kovačič 1994). A common conclusion of these studies has been that

Name of programme: *How Do They Do That?* (Magazine)

Time (secs)	0.92									5.52
Speech	The swimmers who jump out of									
	the water and land perfectly on the top row to become lampladies -									
	how do they do that?									
Time (secs)	0.00									8.12
Subtitle	The swimmers who jump out of									
	the water and land on the top row -									
	how do they do that?									
Time (secs)		2.01	2.24	2.54	2.92	3.56	4.40	5.12	5.92	7.04	8.08
Image	Swimmer in pool	Swimmer in mid-air	Swimmer somersaulting	Swimmer landing	Man in water throwing ball	Woman catches ball	Woman misses ball	Onlooker hits ball	Woman catches ball	Woman with ball	Man in studio

Table 8: Data Record of a Subtitle with Numerous Shot Changes

language serving an interpersonal function is liable to be omitted. This in part provides anexplanation for the relative omission rates in Figure 14, while it should also be remembered that nearly all programmes contain a mixture of discourse styles.

The degree of editing is determined by a wide range of variables, including speech rates, shot changes, text complexity, location of speaker, and screen action. Figure 14 shows how all programme types, with the exception of film, contained a marked degree of editing (ranging from an average of one to eight words per subtitle).

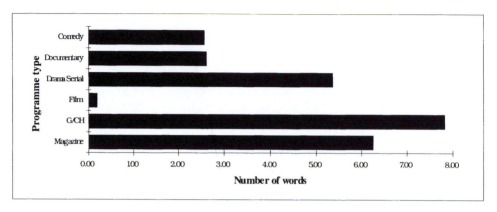

Figure 14: Mean Difference between the Number of Words Spoken and Subtitled

6.5   Summary

This chapter has described how a cross-section of subtitled television was recorded and analyzed in order to examine the characteristics of broadcast subtitles in a range of programme types. Three main features have been considered: synchronicity between subtitle and sound (based on speech and subtitle rates, on-set and off-set times), synchronicity between image and subtitle (based on shot changes), and degree of editing (based on the number of word omissions between dialogue and subtitles). Table 9 summarizes the main characteristics.

Total number of subtitles = 262	Speech rate (wpm)	Subtitle rate (wpm)	On-set time (secs)	Off-set time (secs)	No. of shot changes	Word difference between sp. & sub.
Comedy	208	125	-0.18	0.48	1.52	2.57
Documentary	195	126	-0.1	0.86	1.23	2.62
Drama serial	231	132	0.16	0.8	2.33	5.36
Film	154	67	0.65	0.4	1.54	0.19
G/Ch show	229	133	0.44	0.5	1.84	7.82
Magazine	218	124	-0.38	0.3	2.38	6.25
Mean figures	205	117	0.1	0.56	1.81	4.14

Table 9: Summary of Characteristics of Subtitled Programmes Broadcast for Adults

The above table shows that, on average, subtitles contained 43% less text than the original dialogues. This necessitated a mean editing rate of approximately three words per subtitle combined with extensions to on- and off-set times.

The differences between programme types can be accounted for by differing discourse modes. Programmes containing large sections of interactive dialogue have higher speech rates than narrative-based programmes. Despite greater editing (a mean of seven words per subtitle), they are also characterized by higher subtitle rates.

Subtitle rates can be eased by text editing or extended on- and off-set times. As described previously, the former method can adversely affect subtitle coherence. Extended on-set and off-set times must also be strictly monitored as synchronicity between images and subtitles is crucial. This is most clearly exemplified in sequences of interactive dialogue where visual information (lip movements, body language, etc.) correspond directly with subtitled utterances. In narrative style programmes, where the source of sound is off screen, image/subtitle synchronicity may be slightly relaxed.

These results show how differences in film and discourse modes might affect approaches to subtitling. Variables such as speech rate, discourse style and source of sound clearly influence the outcome of subtitles. Future research may reveal how comprehension is affected in specific contexts: whether there are critical on- and off-set times for particular film and discourse variables the effect on comprehension if these limits are exceeded and the effects of extensive editing. For the present, it is important to be aware of these issues when considering subtitles.

The following chapter continues with an analysis of current programme output by examining subtitled programmes for children.

Chapter Seven: Subtitling for Children

7.1   Introduction

Children's subtitles differ from those for adults because of the distinct linguistic abilities of the two groups. In general, children's subtitles have to be displayed for longer, entailing more editing of the dialogue in order to keep them within the original structure of a programme. This process is by no means straightforward. As illustrated previously (c.f. chapter four), any degree of editing can alter the original meaning of an utterance and affect comprehension.

It has been proposed that subtitle display times should vary in inverse proportion to the age of viewers, as younger children have typical slower reading rates. A recent study (Padmore 1994) showed that subtitles at 90 words per minute were too fast for deaf children aged between eight and fifteen and that their comprehension significantly increased with slower subtitles. Sixty words per minute was considered to be the most effective speed. As it is almost impossible to edit dialogue further, this speed would have to be a starting point for the youngest viewers. However, it is important to note that these display times do not take into account differences in text complexity. Clearly five complex words shown for three seconds would be harder to process than five simple words presented for the same period.

It is likely that subtitle comprehension is also influenced by other factors. Relevance between picture and caption is thought to be significant in improving comprehension. It has also been suggested that strict synchronicity should be maintained between picture and caption, even to the point of losing synchronicity with a soundtrack (Padmore 1994). A viewer's familiarity with subtitled television is another factor thought to affect comprehension (d'Ydewalle et al. 1988).

As with the previous analysis of adult subtitles, no study has yet produced base-line measures of the characteristics of children's subtitles. This chapter provides an analysis of the important features of current subtitles broadcast for children on British television. The following variables were recorded:

- Synchronicity between subtitle and dialogue (including speech rates, subtitle rates, lead and lag times)
- Synchronicity between image and subtitle (i.e. shot changes)
- Extent of editing

7.2   Subtitle samples

A representative set of samples were produced by recording six hours of television on a daily basis over a period of one month (23 May 1994 to 30 June 1994), between 12:30hrs and 17:30hrs (excluding weekends).

Table 10 shows a selection of programmes subtitled for children (broadcast between 12.30hrs and 17.30hrs) on the four main channels. A different channel was recorded each day in order to produce a representative set of samples for British terrestrial television.

The proportion of programmes subtitled for children was remarkably low (only 16 out of 56 programmes, or 29%) compared to the proportion subtitled for adults (135 out of 218 programmes, or 62%) analyzed in the previous chapter. Related to channel, the greatest number of subtitled programmes were broadcast on BBC1 (11 programmes), followed by HTV (five programmes). BBC2 and CH4 did not broadcast any programmes subtitled for children within the time-slot chosen for the study.

	Monday	Tuesday	Wednesday	Thursday	Friday
BBC1	*The New Adventures of Black Beauty* (25mins) *Blue Peter* (25mins)	*The Adams Family* (25mins) *Active 8* (25mins)	*Peter Pan and the Pirates* (25mins) *Hartbeat* (25mins) *Byker Grove* (25mins)	*The House of Gristle* (25mins) *Blue Peter* (30mins)	*The Movie Game* (25mins) *Clowning Around* (25mins)
BBC2	-	-	-	-	-
HTV	*Brill* (20mins)		*Three Seven Eleven* (30mins)	*Animaniacs* (25mins) *The Lodge* (25mins)	*Oasis* (30mins)
CH4	-	-	-	-	-

Table 10: A Representative Set of Programmes Subtitled for Children

7.3   Selection and analysis procedure

Owing to the small number of subtitled programmes, the sample set was not proportioned according to programme type. The duration of each sample was two minutes. The programmes selected were as follows:

Programme Title	Number of Samples (Total = 104)
Black Beauty (film) BBC1	15
Blue Peter (magazine) BBC1	15
Byker Grove (drama serial) BBC1	17
Hartbeat (magazine) BBC1	17
Animaniacs (cartoon) HTV	22
Peter Pan (cartoon) BBC1	18

Table 11: Sample Programmes Subtitled for Children

Dialogue, subtitle, and image features were analyzed in the same way as in the previous chapter. Synchronicity between subtitle and sound was based on the following measurements: duration of speech, duration of associated subtitle, 'lead-in' time of speech to subtitle (i.e. the delay after a speech utterance for a corresponding subtitle), and 'lag' time (i.e. the continuation of a subtitle after a corresponding speech utterance).

The synchronicity between subtitles and images was based on the number of shot changes per subtitle. The extent of editing was measured by the difference in the number of words between a section of speech and a corresponding subtitle.

7.4   Results

7.4.1 Synchronicity between subtitles and sound

Both speech and subtitle rates were relatively slower in children's programmes than in adult programmes (i.e. subtitles were displayed for longer). These differences were expected as both dialogue and subtitles have to be designed for younger viewers. Across a sample of 104 subtitles, speech rates averaged at 186 wpm (19 wpm, or 9.3%, slower than the average rate for adult programmes), while subtitle display rates averaged at 91 wpm (27 wpm, or 23%, slower than adult programmes).

The average subtitle display rate was half the average speech rate. This was achieved by extended lead and lag times and/or greater editing of the dialogue (Figure 15).

Figures 16 and 17 show the on-set and off-set times between speech and subtitles in the sample set of children's programmes. The central line at '0' seconds marks the start and end of speech respectively.

The most striking aspect of Figure 16 is the lack of consistency among the samples. In some samples, subtitles appeared on average a split second after the onset of speech while in others on-set times were just over the maximum limit of 1.5 seconds set by the BBC.

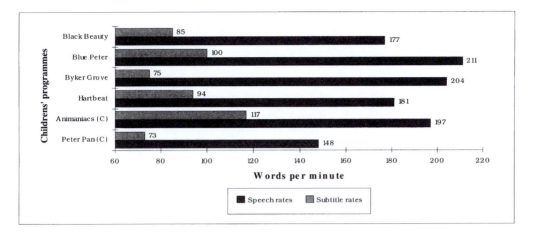

Figure 15: Speech and Subtitle Display Rates

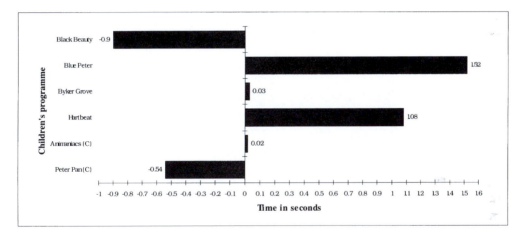

Figure 16: Mean On-set Times between Speech and Subtitles

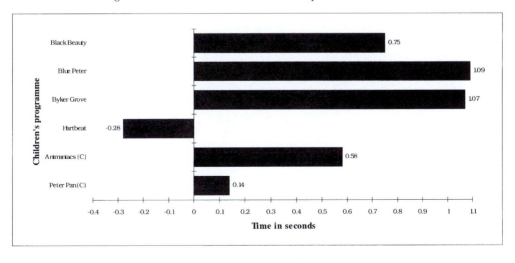

Figure 17: Mean Off-set Time between Speech and Subtitles

The variation between samples may in part be related to source of speech, i.e. on- or off-screen. In both *Blue Peter* and *Hartbeat* there was a high proportion of voice over narration, meaning that subtitles were not tied to speaker's lips and facial movements. Longer delays were therefore perhaps admissible because they caused less frustration. Nevertheless, this apparent flexibility may be deceptive as subtitles still have to synchronize with visual information on screen.

Off-set times were fairly consistent among the sample of children's programmes, with average subtitle display times only falling short of average speech times in one programme, *Hartbeat*. Mean off-set times were the same in both samples of adult and children's programmes, again with the exception of *Hartbeat*.

7.4.2 Synchronicity between subtitles and image
As with adult programmes, the majority of subtitles over-ran at least one shot change (56%). Programmes with more interactive dialogue involving frequent cuts between speakers (e.g. *Black Beauty* and *Peter Pan*) had a greater number of shot changes per subtitle than more narrative style programmes such as *Hartbeat*. The sample from *Animaniacs* had markedly fewer shot changes because of an exceptionally long shot (over a minute) featuring a jaded tom-cat being bored by a garrulous party-goer (Figure 18).

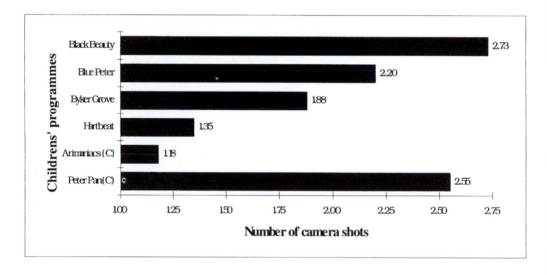

Figure 18: Mean Number of Camera Shots per subtitle

7.4.3 Extent of editing
Figure 19 shows the mean difference in number of words between speech and subtitles. Owing to greater time constraints, imposed by slower reading rates, there was a greater amount of editing in children's programmes (a mean omission rate of seven words as opposed to four in adult programmes).

Among the children's programmes, *Hartbeat* had a particularly large number of single word omissions. Again, this probably related to the nature of the programme sequence which included descriptions of paintings that were also visible on screen. This overlap perhaps relaxed the need to subtitle as much spoken information.

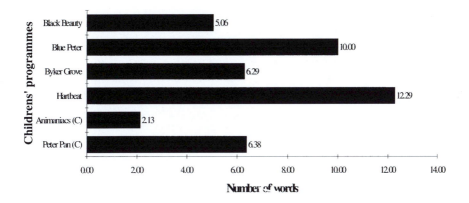

Figure 19: Mean Difference in Number of Words Spoken and Subtitled

7.5   Summary

As explained in the introduction, a cross section of British television was selected, recorded and analyzed to produce baseline measurements of children's subtitled programmes. Table 12 illustrates the key parameters for the sample of children's subtitled television broadcast over a one-month period (23 May 1994 to 30 June 1994), between 12:30 and 17:30hrs.

The figures provide a clear description of current subtitle output and give an indication of relations between individual variables. For example, the relationship between subtitle rate and linguistic variation between speech and subtitles. It can be seen from Table 12 that programmes with faster subtitle rates (e.g. *Animaniacs*, 117 wpm) tend to have less editing of the source dialogue. Likewise, both *Peter Pan* (73 wpm) and *Byker Grove* (75 wpm) which had compara-tively slower subtitle rates displayed a greater degree of editing of the source dialogue.

The only exception appeared to be *Blue Peter*, with relatively fast subtitle rates and a large number of omissions from the source dialogue. This can be explained with reference to the speech rate, which was considerably faster than in other programmes. Consequently, in order to produce appropriate subtitle rates there had to be a greater amount of word omissions and increased on-set and off-set times. These kinds of adjustments may affect readability as mis-matches between image and subtitle due to over-stretched on-set and off-set times are thought to disrupt comprehension (Baker et al. 1984).

It is instructive to see comparative measurements of subtitles broadcast for children and adults. Table 13 lists the mean values of the key parameters.

Looking at table13, it is clear that subtitles in adult programmes are not as constrained as subtitles in children's programmes, in the sense that there is a smaller gap between the original speech rates and subtitle rates. The average subtitle rate for children, 90 wpm, far exceeds the recommended subtitle rate of 60 wpm for children aged between 8 and 15 years old (Padmore 1994). Further reductions in subtitle rates would either entail an even greater number of word omissions per subtitle (currently averaging seven), or an extension of on- and off-set times. The latter adjustment might affect readability, as described above.

Clearly more research needs to be done to assess the relative effects of specific subtitle characteristics. Should linguistic content be sacrificed for strict on-set and off-set times? Do longer delays affect text comprehension? Are there particular features of subtitles which specifically affect reading behaviour? The following chapter looks more closely at the relationship between medium and viewer through a series of eye-movement experiments designed to monitor viewers while they watch subtitled television.

Total no. of subtitles =104	Speech rate (wpm)	Subtitle rate (wpm)	On-set time (secs)	Off-set time (secs)	No. of shot changes	Word difference between sp. & sub.
Black Beauty	177	85	-0.9	0.75	2.73	5.06
Blue Peter	211	100	1.52	1.09	2.20	10
Byker Grove	204	75	0.03	1.07	1.88	6.29
Hartbeat	181	94	1.08	-0.28	1.35	12.29
Animaniacs	197	117	0.02	0.58	1.18	2.13
Peter Pan	148	73	-0.54	0.14	2.55	6.38
Mean figures	186	90	0.2	0.56	1.98	7.03

Table 12: Summary of Characteristics of Subtitles Broadcast for Children

Children's programmes (n=104) Broadcast between 12:30hrs & 17:30hrs	Adult programmes (n=262) Broadcast between 17:30hrs & 23:30hrs
Speech rates (approximately 186 wpm)	Speech rates (approximately 205 wpm)
Subtitle rate (approximately 90 wpm)	Subtitle rate (approximately 117 wpm)
On-set times (0.2 secs)	On-set times (0.1 secs)
Off-set times (0.56 secs)	Off-set times (0.56 secs)
Number of shot changes (1.98)	Number of shot changes (1.81)
Number of word omissions (mean of 7)	Number of word omissions (mean of 4)

Table 13: Comparison of Subtitles for Children and Adults

Chapter Eight: Analyzing Viewing Behaviour

8.1   Introduction

The previous two chapters have described the features of subtitled programmes broadcast for adults and children on British television. The purpose of this chapter is to present the results of a series of experiments, examining how particular features of subtitled programmes affect reading behaviour.

As noted in chapter five, a range of methods have been used to study the effectiveness of subtitles. The few eye movement experiments that have been conducted have been valuable in providing information about the dynamic properties of subtitling which affect the reading process. Most research has been carried out on foreign language subtitling (d'Ydewalle and Vanderbeeken 1996; d'Ydewalle et al. 1987, 1988; d'Ydewalle and Van Rensbergen 1989; Gielen and d'Ydewalle 1992; Verfaillie and d'Ydewalle 1987) while a small pilot study was conducted some years ago at Southampton University (Baker 1982) on intralingual subtitles.

The features of subtitles considered to have a marked affect on reading include some of those examined in the previous two chapters:

- Subtitle rate (speed at which subtitles are displayed).
- Lead times (time at which subtitles appear after the onset of speech).
- Shot changes (number of shot changes occurring with a subtitle).
- Extent of editing (number and type of omissions from the source utterance).
- Visibility of speaker (whether a speaker is on- or off-screen).

This list is based partly on previous research and partly on practical experience. There are undoubtedly other aspects of subtitling which affect reading behaviour such as various film devices but, at present, the features listed above are considered to be some of the most significant.

It is important to stress at this point that 'reading' is a complex process, only part of which can be revealed through eye movement analysis (c.f. chapter three). However, as eye movements indicate how people visually process written text, they are a significant source of empirical information about how people 'read' in practice (Rayner and Pollatsek 1989). Therefore, the terms 'reading' and 'reading behaviour' are used in this chapter when referring to viewers' eye movements.

The relationship between eye movements and 'reading' is perhaps best illustrated by analogy with other cognitive tasks involving visual stimuli. For example, eye movement experiments have also been used to study chess playing (Analyse 1986, c.f. Figures 26 and 27).

8.1.1 Experimental procedure

Five experiments were carried out to examine the effects of the above subtitle features on reading behaviour, through analyzing deaf and hearing viewers' eye movement patterns when presented with different types of subtitled programmes.

8.1.1.1 Participants

The experiments were carried out with the help of a group of 20 volunteers, made up equally of deaf and hearing people. The average age of the hearing people was 29.7 years while the average age of the deaf people was 33.7 years. No volunteer was aged under 21 or over 55 years. Among the deaf people, there were six men and four women while among the hearing people, there were six women and four men. Eight deaf people had profound hearing loss

(91+ decibels) while the remaining two had between 66-90 decibels hearing loss. Nine deaf people had learnt to sign during childhood.

Reading abilities among the group were assessed by inviting volunteers to complete questionnaires on their reading habits. An initial proposal, to carry out reading tests, had to be discarded due to the lack of any general reading test suitable for both deaf and hearing people. The difficulties in designing such reading tests have been well documented (Davidson and Green 1988, Webster 1986). A major problem lies in the wide discrepancy between the complex processes involved in reading and the techniques used to measure them. An assessment of reading experience (of both print and screen based material) was a viable solution for the proposed study.

Responses to the questionnaires showed that hearing participants watched on average 1-5 hours of non-subtitled television a week, whereas deaf participants watched between 11-20 hours of subtitled television a week, plus an additional 1-5 hours of non-subtitled television (e.g. sport). Regarding the print based material, hearing participants read more frequently (once a day) than deaf participants (once a week). However, deaf participants were more likely to read magazines and journals (c.f. Appendix Four). This tendency was considered significant in the context of the study as magazines and journals contain a higher proportion of visual material.

8.1.1.2 Materials
Ten short video clips, each lasting two minutes, were selected from programmes shown on the major British terrestrial channels (c.f. Appendix One). The video clips were coded into pairs, according to contrasting subtitle features. Five features were examined in separate studies.

Studies of subtitle features	Programme titles
Study one: Subtitle Rate 1a. Fast subtitle rate (mean 139wpm) 1b. Slow subtitle rate (mean 74wpm)	*Horizon* (BBC2) *How Do They Do That?* (BBC1)
Study two: Onset of speech 2a. Onset of speech precedes subtitle (mean 0.8secs) 2b. Onset of speech follows subtitle (mean 0.02secs)	*Brookside* (CH4) *Eastenders* (BBC1)
Study three: Shot changes 3a. Low number of shot changes (mean 1.3) 3b. High number of shot changes (mean 3.5)	*In Search of Our Ancestors* (BBC2) *How Do They Do That?* (BBC1)
Study four: Extent of editing 4a. More word omissions per subtitle (mean 9.6) 4b. Fewer word omissions per subtitle (mean 2.4)	*Oprah Winfrey* (CH4) *Absolutely Fabulous* (BBC1)
Study five: Visibility of speaker 5a. Speaker on-screen 5b. Speaker off-screen	*News* (HTV) *News* (HTV)

Table 14: Subtitle Features

T-tests were carried out on all ten clips to verify that each pair only differed according to the feature being examined. The results confirmed that all other features were distributed randomly over each pair.

Participants' eye movement patterns were recorded by an eye gaze monitor (EMR-V, see Figure 20).

The EMR-V incorporates a small solid-state television image device which is displayed in the monitor and records onto video tape the eye marks in motion. For a full description of the equipment and its operation, see *NAC Eyemark Recorder Model V* (1995). Figure 21 displays a three-second sample of a participant's eye movements.

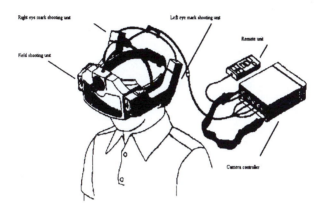

Figure 20: EMR-V Eye Gaze Monitor

8.1.2 Procedure

All volunteers were informed that they would be participating in research on television subtitles. Each participant was tested individually, watching ten two-minute video clips. All the video clips shown to both deaf and hearing participants had the sound turned off. A brief description was given before each clip of the programme from which it was extracted (either orally or in sign language). Participants were asked to watch the programme excerpts in the same way as they would at home. The order of the video clips was rearranged for each participant. While watching the video clips, participants' eye movement patterns were recorded by the eye gaze monitor (EMR-V, see Figure 20). An initial practice video clip was shown before commencing with the experimental material.

For each subject the following measurements were recorded (c.f. Appendix Three):

- Reading time – time taken to read each word (i.e. time between first and last fixation divided by number of words)
- Deflections – number of times a viewer's eyes deflected away from the subtitle area to focus on the image
- Duration of deflections
- Fixations – number of words per fixation.
- Regressions – number of times participants re-read words or characters
- Re-reading – number of times participants re-read an entire subtitle

The first and last 30 seconds of each video clip were not included in the analysis, leaving a one-minute time sample of each participant's eye-movements. Participants were given a series of comprehension questions after each video clip and also asked about their impressions of the experiment (either orally or in sign language).

Certain eye movement features were not included in the analysis, for example duration of fixations and length of saccades. Nevertheless, the features listed above were sufficient to give a good indication of reading behaviour. It is important to note that features of reading behaviour cannot be simply categorized as either positive or negative. For example, it might be assumed that re-reading a subtitle is superfluous and therefore a negative feature. Yet in certain circumstances, such as when a subtitle refers to something specific, the meaning of the text may only become apparent after referring to the image and then re-reading the subtitle. The aim of eye-movement research is therefore to consider features of viewing behaviour in context, in order to make better judgements about the effects of specific subtitle features.

Figure 21: Three-second Sample of a Participant's Eye Movements
BBC (March 1994) Absolutely Fabulous, 'Poor'
(Subtitle font modified for clarity).

Participants' eye-movement patterns were analyzed in terms of the following variables: whether a participant was deaf or hearing; type of programme; specific subtitle features. Because authentic programme excerpts were used for the experiments, the results are immediately relevant to actual television subtitling. However, the benefits in using such material have to be weighed against a certain amount of reduced control over programme content. While T-tests were carried out to confirm the random distribution of all subtitle features (other than the one being examined), using authentic material necessarily means that programme content varies with each programme excerpt. The alternative is to manufacture contrasting subtitles for the same programme, but as the study was aimed at examining actual subtitles this method was not adopted.

8.2   Results and analysis

The results of each study are described below, including a discussion of the significant effects of the *independent variables* (group, programme and subtitle) on the *dependent variables* (reading time, number of deflections, duration of deflections, words per fixation, number of regressions, and re-reading). Differences between the reading behaviour of deaf and hearing people are only referred to if they were shown to be significant. Thus, if no mention is made of 'group', the results apply to deaf and hearing participants alike.

A multi-factor ANOVA design was used for all five studies. The factors were group, programme and subtitle. The first two factors contained two levels: group (deaf/hearing); programme (contrasting features). The number of levels in the third variable, subtitle (n=x), varied in each study. The factorial designs were as follows:

Study 1	2 x 2 x 12
Study 2	2 x 2 x 12
Study 3	2 x 2 x 18
Study 4	2 x 2 x 26
Study 5	2 x 2 x 19

The varying levels of the third factor are a result of differing numbers of subtitles contained in the programme excerpts used for each experiment. The number of subtitles also had to be normalized for each pair of excerpts. For example, in the first experiment two programme excerpts were chosen with contrasting subtitle rates, the 'slow rate' programme having fewer subtitles per minute than the 'fast rate' programme. As both programmes in the study were required to have an identical number of subtitles, the number of subtitles in the 'fast rate' programme had to be reduced to match the number of subtitles in the 'slow rate' programme, hence the low level of factorial design in the first study.

8.2.1 Study one: subtitle rate

The first study examined the effects of fast and slow subtitle rates on reading behaviour. It was assumed that programmes with faster subtitle rates would be more difficult to read. Although reading time and the number of words per fixation were expected to reflect the pace of subtitles, it was assumed that more information would be retained from slower subtitles, especially with deaf participants. In addition, it was expected that more re-reading would occur with slower subtitles as more reading time was available.

Programme 1a – Fast subtitle rate (mean 139 wpm)
Programme 1b – Slow subtitle rate (mean 74 wpm)

Results showed that there was a significant interactive effect of the two independent variables, programme and subtitle, on: *reading time* ($F(5,90)=10.64$, $p<.0000$); *fixations* ($F(5,90)=2.64$, $p<.0285$); and *re-reading* ($F(5,90)=3.20$, $p<.0106$).

8.2.1.1 Interactive effects of programme and subtitle

Reading time

Reading time differed significantly in both programmes. On average less time was spent on words (0.25 secs/word) in programme 1a with fast subtitles than in programme 1b with slow subtitles (0.3 secs/word). This suggests that reading time is reflected in the pace of subtitles.

Reading time also differed with contrasting subtitle rates. The main interactive effect appeared to be due to the presence of two one-word subtitles ('APPLAUSE') in programme 1b, each displayed for around 0.6 seconds. In both instances more time was taken to read these one word subtitles (mean 0.43 secs/word) than was taken with other words in normal full-sentence subtitles. This was most probably due to the additional time available to read them and reinforces the view that reading time varies with subtitles and has a major effect on re-reading.

Fixations

The number of words per fixation was consistent with the above data pertaining to the number of words processed per second. Participants processed more words per fixation (1.36 word/ fixation) in programme 1a than in programme 1b (1.33 word/fixation). The interactive effect of programme and subtitle, however, does not appear to be due to the 'APPLAUSE' subtitles, but to another instance in programme 1b where the number of words per fixation among deaf participants was almost double that of hearing participants. The subtitle reads:

> None of that would be possible
> without Care For The Wild
> Their Chairman is Bill Jordan

There are a number of features of this subtitle which may have affected processing time, including context. It was preceded by a six second subtitle ('APPLAUSE') with a scene-shift from an embedded film clip back to a television studio, suggesting a topic closure. As the above subtitle reinvokes an unspecificied topic through the use of *that*, extra time may have been taken searching for a reference if it had been construed deictically. If this was the case, it exemplifies something of potentially wider significance as anaphoric elements are such a major part of language. The subtitle is also potentially ambiguous, containing the noun phrase 'Care For The Wild'. Despite the capital letters, the first word, 'Care', can either be read as part of a proper noun (i.e. the name of an organization) or as part of a declarative statement.

Despite the textual complications, deaf participants processed twice as many words per fixation as hearing participants. However, this did not appear to reflect ease of comprehension: forty per cent of hearing participants were able to name the organization helping elephants, compared with twenty per cent of deaf participants. This may suggest that hearing participants spent greater time resolving the ambiguous content. If ambiguity does have a significant effect on comprehension it is also of potentially great significance, as it is again such a pervasive feature of language.

Re-reading

Considerably more re-reading occurred in programme 1b (0.615) than in programme 1a (0.315). As anticipated, the main interactive effect of programme and subtitle resulted from longer display times. The most re-reading occurred with the following subtitle which was displayed for 8.56 seconds:

> The elephants are transferred
> to a kind of holding pen
> to acclimatise them

Apart from the reduction of the intentional phrase (*in order to* → *to*), which may have produced confusion, re-reading was most probably caused by a long display time. The lack of detail in the image may have also been a contributory factor as the shot was almost entirely in darkness, showing a vague outline of two huts serving as holding pens.

Average comprehension scores for programme 1b were far lower (46%) than for programme 1a (71%) with quicker subtitles. This went against expectations as it had been assumed that comprehension would be aided by slower subtitles. These scores might have resulted from the contrasting visual content of the programme excerpts. While both programmes were documentaries, more emphasis was placed on textual information in programme 1a, with an almost opposite relation in programme 1b. This difference in levels of visual and textual information was highlighted in one participant's comments:

> In programme 1b one is more conscious of what is happening in the film rather than the subtitles, maybe because of the subject matter. Also there is less concrete information to take in from the subtitles.

8.2.2 Study two: onset of speech

The second study examined the effects of speech preceding or following the start of a subtitle. It was expected that there would be an effect on the number of deflections. If speech followed subtitles, it was anticipated that the number of deflections would increase as viewers sought to locate a speaker. It was also considered that re-reading might occur for the same reason.

> Programme 2a – Onset of speech preceding subtitle (mean 0.8 secs)
> Programme 2b – Onset of speech following subtitle (mean 0.0 secs)

The results showed significant main effects on *re-reading* by group $(F(1,18)=13.50, p<.0017)$, programme $(F(1,18)=7.24, p<.0149)$, and subtitle $(F(7,126)= 4.61, p<.0001)$. In addition there was also a significant interactive effect of programme and subtitle on the number of *deflections* $(F(7,126)=27.54, p<.00000)$.

8.2.2.1 Main effects of group, programme and subtitle

Re-reading
As stated above, there were three main effects on re-reading: group, programme and subtitle. In general, hearing participants re-read subtitles twice as frequently as deaf participants (mean for hearing group 0.48; mean for deaf group 0.24). As hearing participants tended to read more quickly more time was available for them to return to a subtitle. Fewer re-readings occurred with programme 2a, where speech preceded subtitles (mean 0.26), in comparison with programme 2b, where speech followed the start of subtitles (mean 0.46). This difference appeared less due to lead times than to the nature of the closing subtitles in programme 2a all of which, contained close dialogue where a second speaker's remarks were added soon after a first speaker's comments. This led to an increase in the number of deflections to the image in order to identify speakers and addressees, leaving viewers less time to re-read an entire subtitle.

The subtitles producing the greatest amount of re-reading did not have uniform lead times. Their common characteristic was the representation of dialogue with only one speaker visible at any time. As noted above, this led to an increase in the number of deflections to the image, thereby leaving less time for re-reading.

8.2.2.2 Interactive effect of programme and subtitle

Deflections
The number of deflections occurring with programme 2a and 2b differed significantly. Participants

displayed a fairly constant number of deflections with programme 2b where speech followed subtitles. However, with programme 2a there was a sharp rise in the number of deflections occurring towards the end of the programme. This was a direct result of the closing subtitles which again contained close dialogue with a second speaker's comments added immediately after those of a first speaker. Some examples are listed below, with the second speaker's comments in italics:

> Ronaldo Dixon, I presume
> *Er, ... Ron Dixon, Compere*

> Ray Piper
> *Stand-in compere*
> And loving it!
> Will you introduce me?

> Pleased to meet you. Like a drink?
> *No thanks*
> C'mon – my table, my guests

As there was no variation in font or colour, viewers had to scrutinize the image and subtitle to establish the identity of any given speaker.

In this respect, the sequence exemplifies an earlier point, that eye-movement patterns must be considered in the full audiovisual context of a programme as viewers have to process a combination of visual and textual information. When sound and visual information are available simultaneously, rapid conversational interchanges do not present a problem, as a viewer can readily associate speaker with speech through voice tone, etc. However, if speaker and speech have to be processed serially through one visual channel as with subtitled television, a viewer's attention is necessarily divided, giving rise to potential confusion.

8.2.3 *Study three: shot changes*
The third study examined the effects of shot changes occurring across subtitles. It was assumed that programmes with a high number of shot changes would disrupt reading behaviour by provoking frequent deflections to the image. It was also supposed that there might be an associated effect on the number of words processed per fixation, the number of regressions and the amount of re-reading.

> Programme 3a – Low number of shot changes (mean 1.3)
> Programme 3b – High number of shot changes (mean 3.5)

The results showed that there was a significant main effect of programme on *duration of deflections* ($F(1,18)=5.75$, $p<.0276$) and a significant interactive effect of programme and subtitle on the following dependent variables:

> *Reading time* $F(8,144) = 20.60$, $p<.0000$
> *Fixations* $F(8,144) = 5.41$, $p<.0000$
> *Regressions* $F(8,144) = 8.42$, $p<.0000$
> *Re-reading* $F(8,144) = 5.21$, $p<.0000$

8.2.3.1   Main effect of programme

Duration of deflections
The duration of deflections differed between programmes 3a and 3b, appearing to confirm the hypothesis that the number of deflections is likely to rise with increasing shot changes. The average duration of deflection with programme 3b, which had a high number of shot changes, was significantly higher (0.21 secs/sub) than with programme 3a which contained fewer shot changes per subtitle.

8.2.3.2   Interactive effect of programme and subtitle

Reading time
Although reading times differed across both programme and subtitle, they did not appear to be affected by shot changes. Average reading times were similar for both programmes: 3a – 0.3 word/secs; 3b – 0.2 word/secs. The slight increase with programme 3a appeared to be caused by a very brief subtitle (*'Archaeologist Rhys Jones'*), where the average reading time doubled.

Fixations
The number of words per fixation differed significantly across programme and subtitle. In contrast to reading times, the number of words per fixation did appear to be influenced by the number of shot changes. Subtitles with a large number of shot changes gave rise to fewer fixations. In an unusual case, where nine shot changes occurred during a single subtitle, the number of words per fixation rose sharply from an average of 1.5 to 2.5 words per fixation. This effect was repeated with another subtitle presented against five shot changes. The rise in the number of words per fixation was consistent for both deaf and hearing participants. Clearly, as more time was spent referring to the screen image, less time was available to read the subtitles. This enforced quicker reading and hence produced a higher number of words per fixation.

Regressions
The number of regressions appeared to reflect reading times, as fluctuations were due to the length of subtitles rather than to shot changes. In the brief subtitle '*Archaeologist Rhys Jones*' the average number of regressions doubled. In this instance, the number of regressions may also have been influenced by participants' knowledge that they were going to be tested. In anticipation of a question either related to Rhys Jones' occupation or indeed his name, more care may have been taken to process this subtitle.

Re-reading
The results confirmed that re-reading is induced by frequent shot changes. Significantly more re-reading occurred with programme 3b (mean 0.47) than with programme 3a which had a relatively low number of shot changes per subtitle (mean 0.28). In addition, the degree of re-reading increased with subtitles covering multiple shot changes. For example, in the case where nine shot changes occurred during a subtitle, average re-readings jumped to 0.9. In the same programme, where there was on average only one shot change per subtitle, the average number of re-readings was 0.05.

8.2.4 Study four: extent of editing
The fourth study examined the effects of word omissions made in the conversion of dialogue to subtitles. It was cautiously supposed that subtitles with a high number of word omissions might be

harder to process because of mismatches between speakers' utterances and subtitles. Thus it was proposed that fewer words might be processed per fixation in the case of highly edited subtitles.

Programme 4a – High number of word omissions (mean 9.6)
Programme 4b – Low number of word omissions (mean 2.4)

The results showed that there were three significant interactive effects of group and programme, group and subtitle, and programme and subtitle.

8.2.4.1   Interactive effect of group and programme
Group and programme effect on *fixations* F(1,18) = 5.63, p<.0290

Fixations
Programme 4a, containing a high number of word omissions, induced lower fixation rates (1.3C wd/fix) than programme 4b which had a low number of word omissions (1.43 wd/fix). In addition, marginally lower fixation rates were recorded for deaf participants (1.3 wd/fx) than for hearing participants (1.4 wd/fix).

8.2.4.2   Interactive effect of group and subtitle
Group and subtitle effects on *reading time* F(12,216)= 2.54, p<.0038; *fixations* F(12,216)= 2.30, p<.0089.

Reading time
The effect of group and subtitle on reading time was not due to editing but rather to the length and time of the subtitles. Reading times among both deaf and hearing viewers rose in only one instance, from an average of 0.3 secs/wd to an average of 1.1 secs/wd. This was undoubtedly due to a peculiar subtitle that had been altered to imitate pronunciation, i.e. '*Cappu-CCI-NO!*'.

On average, reading times for deaf participants were marginally lower (0.29secs/wd.) than for hearing participants (0.27 secs/wd.). However, overall reading times fluctuated with subtitle rates, similar to the first study.

Fixations
As noted above, fewer words per fixation were recorded with programme 4a (mean 1.30 wd/fix), which contained larger amounts of edited text, than with programme 4b (mean 1.43 wd/fix). Deaf participants also displayed fewer words per fixation (1.3 wd/fix) than hearing participants (1.4 wd/fix). Subtitles showing the greatest degree of editing (around 26/27 words) were associated with the lowest words per fixation rates for both deaf and hearing groups.

8.2.4.3   Interactive effect of programme and subtitle
Programme and subtitle effect on:

Reading time	F(12,216)=	36.46, p<.0000
Deflections	F(12,216)=	12.41, p<.0000
Duration of deflections	F(12,216)=	31.35, p<.0000
Fixations	F(12,216)=	6.41, p<.0000
Re-reading	F(12,216)=	3.01, p<.0006

Reading time
As noted previously, the effect of group and subtitle on reading time did not appear to be due to the degree of editing but rather to the length and presentation time of a subtitle. In the rare case where a subtitle contained a truncated word, reading times among deaf and hearing viewers rose from an average of 0.3 secs/wd to 1.1 secs/wd.

Duration of deflections
The number and duration of deflections differed significantly between programme 4a and programme 4b. However, the differences did not appear related to the extent of editing. Programme 4a gave rise to wide ranging deflection readings, alternating between high and low. For example, the number of deflections was high for both deaf and hearing viewers when viewing subtitles 3,5,7,9, whereas no deflections at all were recorded for subtitles 4,6,8,10. A probable explanation for this alternate pattern is that due to the speed and content of the excerpt viewers did not have sufficient time to look at both subtitle and image in every camera shot. Therefore, the subtitles could only be processed alternately.

The deflections recorded for programme 4b displayed a similar pattern but they were fewer in total with a minimal average duration (0.25 secs, compared with 1.5 secs for programme 4a).

Fixations
As noted above, both deaf and hearing viewers processed fewer words per fixation with programme 4a (1.30 wd/fix) than with programme 4b (1.43 wd/fix) which contained less editing. This may have resulted from confusion caused by a greater degree of mismatches between speakers' silent moving mouths and the subtitles. There was also more visual activity in general; the programme excerpt featuring a live studio discussion with a packed audience.

Re-reading
Programme 4a with more highly edited text induced less re-reading (mean 0.19), than programme 4b (mean 0.25). As lower fixation rates were recorded for programme 4a it would follow that slightly less time would be available for re-reading.

8.2.5 Study five: visibility of speaker
The fifth study examined the effects of subtitles with a speaker either on- or off-screen (c.f. Figure 22, Figure 23). It was assumed that subtitled programmes with a visible static speaker would be easier to follow as viewers could simply focus on the subtitle area and the speaker's lip movements. Conversely, sequences with an off-screen speaker and active images were expected to be more difficult to follow, resulting in longer deflections away from the subtitle and leaving less reading time.

Programme 5a – Speaker off-screen
Programme 5b – Speaker on-screen

The results showed one significant main effect of group and two significant interactive effects of group and programme, and programme and subtitle.

8.2.5.1 Main effect of group
Group effect on: *Duration of deflections* $F(1,18)= 4.48$, $p<.0484$

Duration of deflections
The deflections recorded for deaf participants were considerably longer (0.06 secs) than those recorded for hearing participants (0.01 secs). Deaf participants also showed longer deflections (approximately 0.3 secs) when viewing excerpts containing an active agent not visible on-screen, e.g.:

> Fire-fighters are being blamed
> for worsening the disaster (Programme 5a)

> Susan Whybrow and Dennis Saunders
> were convicted three years ago (Programme 5b)

These types of subtitles appeared to cause a visual 'garden-path' effect as participants attempted to locate the agents in the image.

8.2.5.2   Interactive effect of group and programme
Group and programme on:

> *Reading time* $F(1,18)= 4.44$, $p<.0493$
> *Regressions* $F(1,18)= 5.81$, $p<.0269$.

Reading time
Average reading times recorded for deaf participants were marginally slower (0.28 secs/wd) than those recorded for hearing participants (0.24 secs/wd). There was also a greater difference in their reading times between the two programme excerpts: 0.25 secs/wd for programme 5a (off-screen speaker) compared with 0.32 secs/wd for programme 5b (on-screen speaker). The difference in reading times for hearing participants across the two programme excerpts was marginal, around 0.02secs/wd.

Regressions
Deaf and hearing groups displayed contrasting patterns of regression. Deaf participants regressed more when viewing programme 5b (0.13 regressions per subtitle (reg./sub.) than when viewing 5a (0.9 reg./sub.) while the opposite was the case for hearing participants (5a: 0.10 reg./sub., 5b: 0.07 reg./sub.). The high number of regressions displayed by deaf participants when viewing programme 5b appeared to be caused by constant deflections to the screen image in order to check lip movements.

8.2.5.3   Interactive effect of programme and subtitle
Programme and subtitle on:

> *Reading time* $F(7,126)= 22.71$, $p<.0000$
> *Number of fixations* $F(7,126)= 9.78$, $p<.0000$
> *Regressions* $F(7,126)= 2.18$, $p<.0399$

Reading time
As noted above average reading times for programme 5a (off-screen speaker) were quicker than for programme 5b (on-screen speaker) particularly among deaf participants. The subtitles inducing the slowest reading times principally differed in length and display time, supporting

earlier results showing that reading time was influenced by subtitle rate (see study one).

Fixations
The average words per fixation rate was marginally greater for programme 5a (1.43 wd/fix) than for programme 5b (1.36 wd/fix). This appeared to be the result of more frequent deflections to the image.

In programme 5b, where there was no action beside the lip movements of the newsreader, participants appeared to alternately focus on subtitle and speaker's expression.

In contrast, participants' eye-movements were more distributed for programme 5a, focusing on numerous elements of the screen image. This led to quicker reading (i.e. more words were processed per fixation) as less time was available to read the subtitles. The difference in eye-movement behaviour was consistent with participants' remarks after the experiment:

> In programme 5b, the newsreader just sat there so it was easier to focus on the subtitles.

> In programme 5a, you don't have time to view the picture. In programme 5b it felt like you had more time to look.

> Programme 5b is easier to understand. The picture is static. In programme 5a, you keep wanting to check the image for any changes.

Regressions
There was a marginal difference between the average rates of regression for programme 5a and 5b (5a: 0.095 reg./sub., 5b: 0.1 reg./sub.). As noted above, there was a significant difference between the average rates recorded for deaf and hearing participants. The subtitles inducing the greatest number of regressions were longer and had shorter display times.

Study and subtitle feature	Reading time	Number of deflections	Duration of deflections	Words per fixation	Regressions	Re-reading
Study 1. Subtitle rate Programme & Subtitle	X			X		X
Study 2. Lead times Group Programme Subtitle Programme & Subtitle		X				X X X
Study 3. Shot changes Programme Programme & Subtitle	X		X	X	X	X
Study 4. Extent of editing Group & Programme Group & Subtitle Programme & Subtitle	X X	X	X	X X X		X
Study 5. Visibility of Speaker Group Group & Programme Programme & Subtitle	X X		X	X	X X	

Table 15: Main and Interactive Effects of Subtitle Features on Reading Behaviour

As a result of increased deflections to the image, there were changes in other features of reading behaviour. Reading time and the number of words per fixation increased as less time was available to process the subtitles. Similarly, the number of regressions decreased as there was opportunity to check words and phrases.

8.3   Summary

Table 15 lists all the main and interactive effects of the examined subtitle features on reading behaviour. The features of reading behaviour affected by the independent variables on the left of the chart are indicated by crosses.

In study one, the main effect of subtitle rate was on reading time. Reading times tended to follow the pace of discourse; quicker subtitle rates induced quicker reading, and vice versa. Subtitles displayed for unusually long periods produced the longest reading times, with very slow subtitles encouraging re-reading.

Comprehension scores (for both deaf and hearing participants) were unexpectedly lower for the slower subtitled programme: an average of forty-six per cent correct answers against seventy-one per cent for the excerpt with faster subtitles. This result could only be explained with reference to the relative content of both excerpts. Although both programmes were documentaries, the programme with faster subtitles contained mainly textual information, while in the programme with slower subtitles far more emphasis was placed on visual content.

The study also highlighted the potential effects of textual ambiguity and anaphora on comprehension. More extensive research into the communicative effects of these components in a subtitling context would be particularly valuable as they are a significant part of language.

In study two, programme content also affected viewing behaviour. The subtitles inducing the greatest amount of re-reading were those representing dialogue where only one speaker was visible at any one time. These sequences necessitated a great number of deflections to the image, leaving less time for re-reading.

This type of filming, where the camera jumps consecutively between speaker and listener, requires subtitles to be displayed within single shots as coordination is essential. However, because linguistic and visual sources have to be received serially through the same visual channel, these sequences are difficult to process.

In study three, shot changes occurring across subtitles were shown to have an influence on deflections and re-reading. Both the duration of deflections and the amount of re-reading increased dramatically in programmes with a high number of shot changes.

Surprisingly, the programme excerpt with more shot changes appeared easier to follow. This was probably due to the content of the programme in which textual and visual information frequently duplicated each other. Therefore information conveyed by the subtitles was also available in the image.

In study four, the most significant effect of word omissions related to the number of words processed per fixation. The programme excerpt with a high degree of word omissions induced lower words per fixation rates among both deaf and hearing groups. This slower reading probably caused, in turn, the low levels of re-reading which were displayed. The lower fixation rates may have been caused by confusion relating to the more numerous mismatches between speakers' silent moving mouths and the subtitles. They may have also resulted from a greater degree of screen activity in general.

In study five, the programme excerpt with an on-screen static speaker appeared to place less processing demands on viewers than the excerpt containing off-screen speakers. The subtitles causing greatest difficulty, particularly for deaf participants, were those relating to an active agent not present in the image. These provoked a visual 'garden-path effect', leading deaf participants to search for an active agent on-screen. Longer deflections to the image caused longer reading times and a greater number of words per fixation. The number of regressions also decreased as less time was available to check words and phrases.

As well as revealing the effects of specific subtitle features, the experiments highlighted the degree to which reading behaviour is affected by visual film features, hinting at the value of further research in this area. Eye-movement research has up till now concentrated on the effects of subtitle features, but it is likely that the visual content of a film is equally important.

Chapter Nine: Conclusions

This book has focused on the various aspects of intralingual subtitling, a medium which plays a vital role in providing deaf and hard-of-hearing people with televised information. Demographic changes leading to a more elderly society mean that an increasing number of people are likely to use subtitled television in future. The number of channels is also likely to grow with the spread of digital television. It is therefore essential to accompany this growth with research assessing the various aspects of the medium.

It is hoped that this book will have partly set new ground by adopting a holistic approach to the subject, considering both semiotic and technical aspects in a range of issues: the linguistic features of subtitles; the reading characteristics of deaf viewers; film conventions and content; the characteristics of current broadcast subtitles and the effects of particular subtitle features on viewing behaviour.

An attempt has also been made to establish the common ground between intra- and interlingual subtitling, as well as other forms of audio-visual language transfer. In the past, these two forms of subtitling have often been viewed separately. Interlingual subtitling has been seen as a derivative of text translation, while intralingual subtitling or 'captioning' has been viewed as a form of editing. The two introductory chapters attempted to challenge these perspectives.

Firstly, as both forms aim to transform dialogue into 'equivalent' text subtitles, they are inevitably amenable, in some part, to similar linguistic theories. The transformation is perceived as more complex in interlingual subtitling as two separate languages are involved, but an attempt has been made to show that even in the case of intralingual subtitling there is a transfer between distinct linguistic systems: spoken dialogue and condensed dynamic written text. Furthermore, performing this transfer involves making linguistic judgements based on complex notions such as *relevance* and *equivalence*.

Secondly, by describing the features of the multimedia environment, this study has tried to show that the same basic conditions apply to both forms: the semiotic interplay between image and text; the material structure of a film and the reading capacities of viewers. The relationship between linguistic and visual content means that neither form of subtitling can be adequately appreciated as simply a linguistic process. In television and film, the two systems are inherently combined.

While both forms of subtitling share the same basic conditions, interlingual subtitles are unsuitable for many deaf viewers owing to high presentation rates and because only the lexical features of a dialogue are transferred into written form. Chapter two introduced the distinctive features of intralingual subtitling, including the additional elements of a soundtrack that are transferred into visual or written form for deaf and hard-of-hearing viewers.

The efficacy of intralingual subtitling partly depends on the reading capacities of its viewers. Chapter three examined the cognitive processes involved in reading, in particular, the re-coding strategies employed by deaf people. The analysis highlighted the marked degree of linguistic diversity among viewers. This diversity raises questions about whether there are universally applicable subtitling standards, in particular, whether a singular presentation rate suits the reading characteristics of all viewers. Significantly, the introduction of digital television means that in future alternative display times may be possible.

While viewers' reading capacities set a limit on subtitle rates, actual reading rates vary with the pace of subtitles, film features and the degree of information being processed from the image. Therefore, it is important to take further account of the relationship between text and film components as well as the basic features and conventions of film production. Chapter four described the integration of linguistic and visual elements and further analyzed the transformation of dialogue into written text. The meaning and comprehensibility of an utterance can be subtly altered when it is condensed into written subtitles. Therefore, the linguistic implications of any omissions should be carefully considered. Often non-content bearing items such as cohesive devices can be as influential as nominal and verbal elements. As dialogue also integrates with the visual content of a film, it would be particularly valuable to conduct further research on exophoric references connecting directly between the two systems.

In addition to affecting the meaning of an utterance, and therefore a film or programme sequence, the transformation of utterances into subtitles also changes the way in which a programme has to be processed by a viewer. When subtitles are substituted for dialogue, linguistic and visual components have to be processed serially through the same visual channel, whereas previously they were able to be processed simultaneously through separate channels. Owing to this change, both sources have to be tightly co-ordinated in order to avoid misreadings. However, certain film sequences still appear to be inherently problematic, such as the shot-reverse-shot convention used with interactive dialogue. It would be valuable to explore film production techniques further, to see if there are further conventions which have a particular bearing on subtitling.

A range of studies have investigated the impact and effectiveness of subtitling. Chapter five described the various approaches taken and the insights which have been gained. Most of these studies have been conducted on intralingual subtitling because of its primary function as a communication aid.

Cumulatively, these studies have emphasized the importance of considering viewers as well as the medium. It is essential to establish that there is no free passage between subtitle and viewer. Research on eye-movement behaviour has clearly illustrated that the way people process subtitles is partly determined by a combination of subtitle and film characteristics, rather than just being a matter of decoding language in written form.

An integral part of examining subtitling is to take account of the features of actual subtitles. Chapters six and seven described the results of a survey of current subtitling on British television for adults and children, analyzing significant features such as standard display times variations according to programme type the synchronization of speech with subtitles and the integration of text and image.

An important finding of the surveys was how features of adult subtitles are partly determined by the type of programme in which they appear due to associated discourse styles. Game and chat shows, for example, have typically higher subtitle rates than documentaries as they are based around interactive discourse. Further research analyzing subtitling in relation to particular programme types would be valuable in revealing greater information about the relationship between subtitling, discourse styles and film content.

In contrast to subtitling for adults, children's programmes have markedly slower subtitle rates owing to children's different reading capacities. Reduced subtitle rates necessarily impose extended lead and lag times and/ or more extensive editing of dialogue. However, both of these alternatives can have adverse effects: shot changes across subtitles can disrupt reading while increased editing can alter meaning and affect coherence. In view of the learning and educational aspect of television, it would be valuable to conduct further research on children's viewing behaviour in order to better inform the stricter editing that takes place. This would complement recent research carried out by the Independent Television Commission (Gregory 1996) on children's comprehension of subtitles.

The way in which subtitles are processed by viewers can be studied quite precisely through an eye-gaze monitor. Chapter eight described a series of experiments investigating the influence of a variety of subtitle features, including subtitle rate, shot changes, lead times, extent of editing and the visibility of speakers. The results revealed a number of effects.

Subtitle rates directly affect reading speed. Faster subtitle rates induce faster reading speeds, and when subtitle rates exceed viewers' reading capacities significant disruption occurs. It was also found that very slow subtitles lead to more re-reading. Lead times appeared to have no direct effect on viewing behaviour, in contrast to film devices such as the shot-reverse-shot convention which were seen to have a marked influence.

Shot changes were discovered to directly influence reading. Numerous shot changes tended to prolong viewers' deflections away from a subtitle and cause an increase in re-reading. The extent of editing was not discovered to directly affect reading behaviour. In contrast, the study indicated the importance of programme content in determining how viewers process subtitles.

Finally, the visibility of a speaker appeared to affect viewing behaviour. Shots in which speakers were not clearly visible induced longer deflections away from the subtitles. Subtitles causing most disruption, particularly among deaf viewers, were those evoking an active agent not visible on screen, prompting a visual 'garden-path' effect. Excerpts containing static visible speakers tended to cause less disruption. These viewing patterns were recorded in relation to a news programme, arguably the prime source of information on television. The excerpt from the programme alternated between static close-up studio shots of a newsreader and external footage shot on location. In the case of the studio shots, deaf viewers made more extensive use of the newsreader's facial cues than hearing viewers. Eye-movement patterns indicated that facial cues were used for a number of purposes: to indicate the start and finish of an utterance; to confirm the wording of a subtitle, and to check unusual words. In the case of location shots, deaf viewers again showed more active eye-movements, appearing to process more content in the image. In view of this difference, it appeared that slower subtitle rates may be more ideal for active location shots and quicker rates for studio presentations with a static newsreader.

A primary aim of this book has been to highlight the multimedia context of subtitled television. While the focus has often been placed on the linguistic aspects of subtitling, eye-movement research has emphasized the degree to which features of the image also affect viewing behaviour. It would be interesting to see the results of further research analyzing eye-movement patterns in relation to film sequences with identical subtitles and contrasting visual content.

Throughout this book, the central premise has been that the multimedia environment of television and film influences subtitling in numerous ways. It is hoped that these influences will have become clear through the various chapters describing text and film aspects of subtitling and the relationship between medium and viewer. By examining certain elements in detail, it is also hoped that this book will have provided useful information for practitioners and stimulated other researchers to address the complex issues which remain to be investigated.

Appendix One: Transcripts of Subtitled Programmes

The following pages contain subtitle tran-scriptions and comprehension questions of the video clips used in Chapter Eight. Information on subtitles and readability accompany each tran-scription. The specific subtitle variable analyzed in each video clip is marked in **bold.**

Trial Study – *Home Truths* (BBC1, 1994)

Liz Smith was born Betty Foster in 1920s Scunthorpe. Acting ambitions were interrupted by the war. Liz joined the WRENS. She toured as a backing singer for Vera Lynn.

After the war, drama school led to work all over London. She had a role in a Greek tragedy, but ... She made the audience laugh so much, she was demoted to spear-carrier!

Liz continued to work in improvisational theatre, but she also worked checking plastic bags for holes. Eventually, Liz got lucky and was snapped up by a famous Broadway theatre company. Liz's work has brought her international recognition, including a BAFTA award in 1985. Finally able to enjoy success, Liz recently learned to drive and she did it in style in a white Rolls-Royce. APPLAUSE

Context:
The following film clip is from a game show about famous people. This clip describes a famous person called Liz Smith.

Detail questions:
1. When was Liz Smith born?
2. When did Liz receive a BAFTA award?
3. Liz learnt to drive in what type of car?

Picture question:
4. What colour dress was Liz wearing at the BAFTA award ceremony?

Concept question:
5. What was Liz's career in?

Answers:
1. 1920
2. 1985
3. Rolls-Royce
4. White
5. Acting/Theatre

Film data	Mean figures	Standard Deviation
Speech rate	168 wpm	37
Subtitle rate	120 wpm	21
Lead time	1.2 secs	1.5
Lag time	1.3 secs	1.2
No. of shot changes	2.2	0.6
No. of word omissions	3	3.1
Source of sound on/off screen	off	

Readability data	Figures	
Passive sentences	12%	
Flesch reading ease	70.7	
Flesch grade level	7.9	
Flesch-Kincaid	4.6	
Gunning fog index	5.1	
Mean words per sentence	15.6	
Mean characters per word	4.6	

Table 16: Film and Readability Data of *Home Truths* (BBC1, 1994)

Study 1a. *Horizon* (BBC2, 1994)

The reality is that these fireball increases will happen suddenly. We have no means of predicting them. They may happen tomorrow, they may happen in 100 years. Who knows? The fact is, we do not, as a world society, have the means of handling this situation at the moment. These grim warnings seem strange given the benign appearance of fireballs.

This one was spotted last year all the way from Canada to Texas. More like a natural firework with a bit of a bang at the end.

REPORTER: Michelle Knapps's car is like a museum exhibit.

People are coming to see the hole in her trunk. What damaged her car was this rock.

She has had calls from collectors wanting to buy it AND the trunk.

Context:
The following film clip is from a documentary about fireballs (meteorites). This clip shows people talking about meteorites.

Detail questions:
1. Can we predict when meteorites will happen?
2. In which area was the meteorite spotted?
3. Where did the meteorite hit Michelle Knapp's car?

Picture question:
4. What colour was Michelle Knapp's car?

Concept question:
5. Why can't we protect ourselves from meteorites?

Answers:
1. No
2. From Canada to Texas
3. On the trunk
4. Red
5. Because we cannot predict when they will happen.

Film data	Mean figures	Standard Deviation
Speech rate	194 wpm	31
Subtitle rate	**139 wpm**	**37**
Lead time	0.0 secs	1.2
Lag time	0.5 secs	0.6
No. of shot changes	1.1	0.3
No. of word omissions	2.7	3.4
Source of sound on/off screen	mixed	
Readability data	**Figures**	
Passive sentences	0%	
Flesch reading ease	86.2	
Flesch grade level	6.4	
Flesch-Kincaid	2.6	
Gunning fog index	5.8	
Mean words per sentence	9.0	
Mean characters per word	4.3	

Table 17: Film and Readability Data of *Horizon* (BBC2, 1994)

Study 1b. *How Do They Do That?*
(BBC1, 1994)

The elephants are transferred to a kind of holding pen to acclimatize them. Finally, they are released into their new home, where the family groups can lead a new life together, safe from the dangers of drought.
APPLAUSE.
None of that would be possible without Care For The Wild.
Their chairman is Bill Jordon.
APPLAUSE.

Context:
This film clip is from a documentary about wildlife. This clip shows elephants being moved to a new habitat.

Detail questions:
1. Where are the elephants transferred to?
2. What is the name of the organization which helps elephants?
3. Who is their chairman?

Picture question:
4. What time (day or night) did they arrive?

Concept question:
5. Why were they in danger at their old home?

Answers:
1. A holding pen
2. Care For The Wild
3. Bill Jordan
4. Night
5. Drought

Film data	Mean figures	Standard Deviation
Speech rate	156 wpm	118
Subtitle rate	**74 wpm**	**53**
Lead time	-0.3 secs	1.7
Lag time	0.0 secs	2.7
No. of shot changes	2.1	0.4
No. of word omissions	3	3.3
Source of sound on/off screen	off	

Readability data	Figures	
Passive sentences	0%	
Flesch reading ease	90.1	
Flesch grade level	6.0	
Flesch-Kincaid	1.9	
Gunning fog index	3.6	
Mean words per sentence	11.0	
Mean characters per word	4.7	

Table 18: Film and Readability Data of *How Do They Do That?* (BBC1, 1994)

Study 2a. *Brookside* (CH4, 1994)

Don't get upset, love, it's your old man I mean.
She can invade my space any time, know what I
mean?
Anyway, I mustn't keep you lot up, so let's have
the first act to audition from the JTC Agency.
Ladies and gentleman, please welcome a great
guy, a name to watch out for, Mr Johnny Laporte!
Flamin' audition night? Why's he letting riff-
raff like that in?
Seems to be going down OK.
Ronaldo Dixon, I presume.
Er, ... Ron Dixon. Compere.
Ray Piper.
Stand-in compere.
And loving it!
Will you introduce me?
Bev.
Pleased to meet you. Like a drink?
No, thanks.
C'mon – my table, my guests.
Oh, your table now, is it?
Slip of the tongue. No offence. Bev?

Context:
This film clip is from a soap opera set in Liverpool.
This clip shows an entertainer at a night-club.

Detail questions:
1. What job does Ronaldo Dixon do?
2. What job does Ray Piper do?
3. What is the name of the woman sitting next to
   Ronaldo Dixon?

Picture question:
4. Was the night-club: crowded, half-full, or empty?

Concept question:
5. Why is Ronaldo Dixon annoyed with Ray Piper?

Answers:
1. Compere
2. Stand-in compere
3. Bev
4. Full
5. He's worried he'll take his job

Film data	Mean figures	Standard Deviation
Speech rate	212 wpm	80
Subtitle rate	136 wpm	21
Lead time	**0.8 secs**	**1.6**
Lag time	1.0 secs	0.8
No. of shot changes	2.2	1.4
No. of word omissions	3.5	3.0
Source of sound on/off screen	off	
Readability data	**Figures**	
Passive sentences	0%	
Flesch reading ease	87.5	
Flesch grade level	6.2	
Flesch-Kincaid	2.1	
Gunning fog index	3.3	
Mean words per sentence	7.6	
Mean characters per word	4.0	

Table 19: Film and Readability Data of *Brookside* (CH4, 1994)

Study 2b. *EastEnders* (BBC1, 1994)

David. Do you want anything?
Depends what you're offering.
I'm looking for my mum.
She ain't been in here. Sit down.
You can find your mum any time.
A bacon butty.
Make it three.
Give us a cuppa. I've just had a drink and it's gone to my head. Sure.
How long have they been here?
Not long. Forget the tea.
Great idea coming round here, Phil.
I saw the Old Bill go into the Jascksons'.
It was still bad idea to come here. How much Scotch have you had?
Not enough.
It's a bit of a giveaway, isn't it?
Everybody has a drink now and then,
What did you tell them? Not a lot.

Context:
This film clip is from a soap opera set in the East End of London. This clip starts in a cafe and then moves to a person's house.

Detail questions:
1. Who is David looking for?
2. Why does the woman entering the cafe want a cup of tea?
3. Where did Old Bill go into?

Picture question:
4. How many people is David sitting with?

Concept question:
5. Why does the girl entering the cafe leave so suddenly?

Answers:
1. His mum
2. She has had a drink
3. Jacksons
4. Two
5. She sees David and the girls.

Film data	Mean figures	Standard Deviation
Speech rate	231 wpm	100
Subtitle rate	133 wpm	22
Lead time	**0.0 secs**	**0.2**
Lag time	0.6 secs	0.6
No. of shot changes	3.1	1.8
No. of word omissions	6.2	5.0
Source of sound on/off screen	on	
Readability data	**Figures**	
Passive sentences	0%	
Flesch reading ease	100	
Flesch grade level	0.0	
Flesch-Kincaid	0.3	
Gunning fog index	3.4	
Mean words per sentence	5.2	
Mean characters per word	3.7	

Table 20: Film and Readability Data of *EastEnders* (BBC1, 1994)

Study 3a. *In Search of Our Ancestors*
(BBC2, 1994)

Each summer, a dedicated excavation team makes the trip to this remote area, miles from any town. Archaeologist Rhys Jones believes the new evidence will undermine the old view that Europe was where modern culture began. This is the remains of a hearth that people once sat around. The team has removed hundreds of stone tools. But when did this happen?
The sand itself provides the answer. These samples are shipped to laser labs to be dated.
Scientist can put a precise time on the appearance of people here.

Context:
This film clip is from a documentary about human ancestry. This clip shows scientists looking for evidence in Australia.

Detail questions:
1. What was the name of the archaeologist?
2. What was discovered in the hearth (fireplace)?
3. Where are the sand samples dated?

Picture question:
4. What does Rhys Jones wear on his helmet?

Concept question:
5. What can the scientist learn from the samples?

Answers:
1. Rhys Jones
2. Stone tools
3. Laser Labs
4. A torch/lamp
5. Where human culture began

Film data	Mean figures	Standard Deviation
Speech rate	189 wpm	41
Subtitle rate	113 wpm	20
Lead time	-0.8 secs	1.0
Lag time	0.9 secs	0.7
No. of shot changes	**1.3**	**0.7**
No. of word omissions	1	1.4
Source of sound on/off screen	off	
Readability data	**Figures**	
Passive sentences	0%	
Flesch reading ease	81.9	
Flesch grade level	6.8	
Flesch-Kincaid	3.1	
Gunning fog index	4.9	
Mean words per sentence	8.1	
Mean characters per word	4.6	

Table 21: Film and Readability Data of *In Search of Our Ancestors* (BBC2, 1994)

Study 3b. *How Do They Do That?*
(BBC1, 1994)

So we shot it so that we had two columns of people falling together, then before they collapsed, we cut to another angle where I wanted the heads to link together. So we put them in harnesses and we had steel bars attached to people at the back, and on cue, they pull them apart, so when we reversed the film, their heads are going together.

The swimmers who jump out of the water and land on the top row – how do they do that?

They were thrown by stunt men and pulled out on kirby-wires.

And the landings? shot in reverse.

They stand on the top of somebody's shoulders, and on cue, they leap forward into a forward roll.

To look like a back somersault, it was actually a front somersault that they reversed.

Context:
This film clip is from a programme which explains technical innovations. This clip shows how an advert for a building society (Halifax) was made.

Detail questions:
1. How were the two columns of people supported?
2. Who threw the swimmers out of the water?

Picture question:
3. What colour was the swimmers' ball?

Concept question:
4. How is a front somersault made to look like a back somersault?

Answers:
1. With harnesses
2. Stunt men
3. Pink
4. It's shown in reverse

Film data	Mean figures	Standard Deviation
Speech rate	248 wpm	26
Subtitle rate	133 wpm	19
Lead time	-0.42 secs	0.7
Lag time	1.1 secs	0.9
No. of shot changes	**3.5**	**2.4**
No. of word omissions	10.3	4.8
Source of sound on/off screen	mixed	
Readability data	**Figures**	
Passive sentences	0%	
Flesch reading ease	85.4	
Flesch grade level	6.5	
Flesch-Kincaid	2.6	
Gunning fog index	5.0	
Mean words per sentence	16.9	
Mean characters per word	4.1	

Table 22: Film and Readability Data of *How Do They Do That?* (BBC1, 1994)

Study 4a. *Oprah Winfrey* (CH4, 1994)

We switched those.

We switched off of medicine that was causing depression. It's a vicious cycle. You start with drug A then drug B, ... then soon you are taking a handful of drugs.

Like this woman over here.

Lady in orange, you had something to say about that. Yea, what was that? I work for a pharmaceutical company.

I sell antibiotics and hypertensive medicines. There are millions of choices. As consumers we have a responsibility to ask the physician. "This isn't working for me". Find out as much about it as you can. The lady who takes 40 pills, ... there are hypertensive drugs that are once a day, ... then the other drugs she has to take because of the side effects. If something is causing you headaches and upset stomach, ... shouldn't you tell your doctor? If we can leave one message, it's pay attention to your body. Talk to your doctor.

Context:
This film clip is from an American chat show. This clip shows a discussion about the misuse of drugs.

Detail questions:
1. Who does the lady in orange work for?
2. What message does the man give to the audience?

Picture question:
3. What colour hair does the lady in orange have?

Concept question:
4. What is the danger of using a drug to combat the side-effects of another drug?

Answers:
1. A pharmaceutical company
2. Pay attention to your body/ Talk to your doctor
3. Blonde
4. You may be taking too many drugs.

Film data	Mean figures	Standard Deviation
Speech rate	250 wpm	81
Subtitle rate	138 wpm	30
Lead time	0.3 secs	0.6
Lag time	0.3 secs	0.5
No. of shot changes	1.3	0.5
No. of word omissions	**9.6**	**8.6**
Source of sound on/off screen	mixed	

Readability data	Figures	
Passive sentences	0%	
Flesch reading ease	80.5	
Flesch grade level	7.0	
Flesch-Kincaid	3.3	
Gunning fog index	5.0	
Mean words per sentence	7.2	
Mean characters per word	4.4	

Table 23: Film and Readability Data of *Oprah Winfrey* (CH4, 1994)

Sample 4b. *Absolutely Fabulous*
(BBC1, 1994)

Cappu-CCI-NO!
All right?
Oh, go on, darling! Make the most of Mummy –
before you run off to be a STUDENT
You've told her. Well done! Though why you'd
want to be a student nowadays ...
No fun, darling. No demos, no experimental
drug-taking. You're just industry fodder! At least
in my day, people went to university just to close
'em down! What will your protest be – stripy
tights and licorice earrings(?)
oh, call out the National Guard (!)
She's just jealous, I could have been a student.
Thick as two short planks, her report said! It did
not say that! It did not!
Ask Patsy, darling.
She wrote most of 'em.
There's no milk.
No milk! Haven't Harrods been yet, darling?
I'll pop out and get some.

Context:
This film clip is from a comedy about a wealthy but
irresponsible woman. This clip shows a conversation
between three woman.

Detail questions:
1. What is the young girl going to be?
2. Who wrote most of 'mummy's' school reports?
3. What have they run out of?

Picture question:
4. Who is smoking?

Concept question:
5. What relation are the three women to each other?

Answers:
1. A student
2. Patsy
3. Milk
4. 'Mummy'
5. Grandmother, mother, daughter

Film data	Mean figures	Standard Deviation
Speech rate	210 wpm	70
Subtitle rate	122 wpm	34
Lead time	-0.2 secs	0.5
Lag time	0.5 secs	0.5
No. of shot changes	1.9	0.9
No. of word omissions	**2.4**	**2.8**
Source of sound on/off screen	mixed	
Readability data	**Figures**	
Passive sentences	0%	
Flesch reading ease	93.8	
Flesch grade level	5.6	
Flesch-Kincaid	1.1	
Gunning fog index	3.5	
Mean words per sentence	6.0	
Mean characters per word	4.2	

Table 24: Film and Readability Data of *Absolutely Fabulous* (BBC1, 1994)

Study 5a. *News* (HTV 1994)

BT says it wants a sharp reduction in the number of its senior managers. It warned of compulsory redundancies if there aren't enough volunteers. A woman and her lover went on trial for a second time today accused of plotting to murder her husband by faking a lawn mower accident. Susan Whybrow and Dennis Saunders were convicted three years ago of conspiring to murder Christopher Whybrow. But the Court of Appeal ruled they hand't had a fair trial.

Context:
This film clip is from the news. This clip is on two news items; job cuts in British Telecom; and a murder case.

Detail questions:
1. Which jobs are to go in British Telecom?
2. Who was accused of murder?
3. How did the murder supposedly happen?

Picture question:
4. Do you see the BT emblem?

Concept question:
5. Did Susan Whybrow and Dennis Saunders have a fair trial three years ago?

Answers:
1. Senior managers
2. A woman and her lover
3. A lawn mower accident
4. Yes
5. No

Film data	Mean figures	Standard Deviation
Speech rate	189 wpm	44
Subtitle rate	174 wpm	81
Lead time	0.7 secs	0.4
Lag time	1.1 secs	0.6
No. of shot changes	1	0.3
No. of word omissions	1.1	2.1
Source of sound on/off screen	**on**	
Readability data	**Figures**	
Passive sentences	0%	
Flesch reading ease	96.6	
Flesch grade level	8.0	
Flesch-Kincaid	5.0	
Gunning fog index	6.1	
Mean words per sentence	6.1	
Mean characters per word	4.6	

Table 25: Film and Readability Data of *News* (HTV 1994)

Study 5b. *News* (HTV 1994)

Dashed in the bow, tons of oil have spewed into the shipping lane.
Firefighters are being blamed for worsening the disaster.
When the ships collided, they sprayed water instead of foam. Which served to spread the oil.
There were fears of a massive slick off Istanbul, but the Turkish government says the danger is past.
The fire on the freighter is out. The vessel drifted towards the shore and ran aground.

Context:
This film clip is from the news. This clip describes the rescue operation of a tanker fire in the Bosphorus (off Turkey).

Detail questions:
1. Where was the tanker dashed?
2. Who is blamed for worsening the disaster?
3. What helped spread the oil?

Picture question:
4. What colour is the tanker?

Concept question:
5. Is the tanker still on fire?

Answers:
1. In the bow
2. The firefighters
3. Water
4. Black and red
5. No

Film data	Mean figures	Standard Deviation
Speech rate	247 wpm	44
Subtitle rate	157 wpm	70
Lead time	-0.06 secs	0.5
Lag time	0.6 secs	0.7
No. of shot changes	1.7	0.7
No. of word omissions	3	2.5
Source of sound on/off screen	**off**	
Readability data	**Figures**	
Passive sentences	0%	
Flesch reading ease	88.8	
Flesch grade level	6.21	
Flesch-Kincaid	2.3	
Gunning fog index	4.0	
Mean words per sentence	5.9	
Mean characters per word	4.6	

Table 26: Film and Readability Data of *News* (HTV 1994)

Appendix Two: Subtitled Video Clips

Figure 22: Speaker Visible on Screen (HTV 1994)

Figure 23: Speaker not Visible on Screen (HTV 1994)

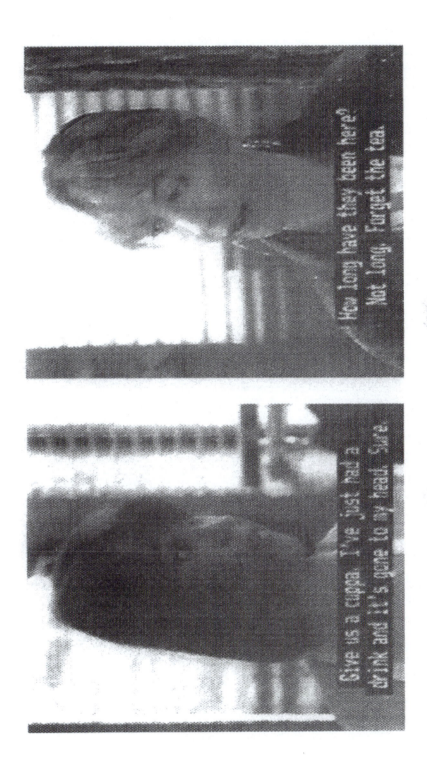

Figure 24: Two Video Clips in Sequence: Shot-reverse-shot Film Convention (BBC1, 1994)

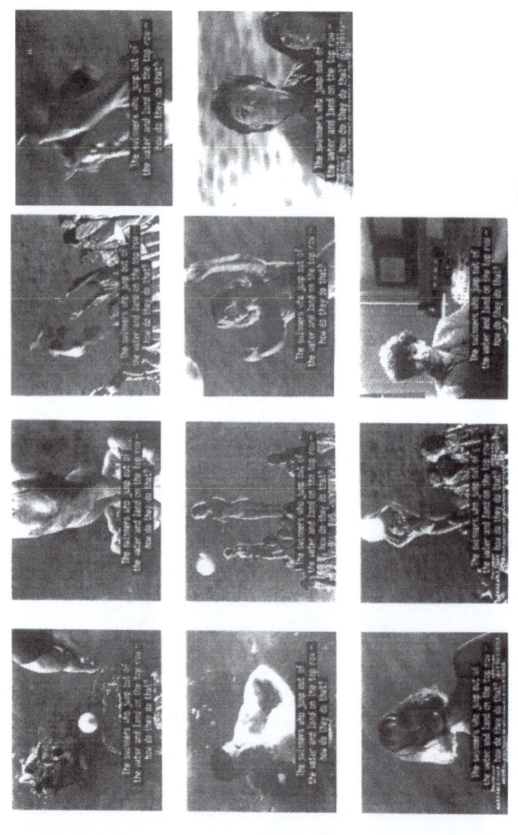

Figure 25: Eleven Video Clips in Sequence: Subtitle with a Large Number of Shot Changes (BBC1, 1994)

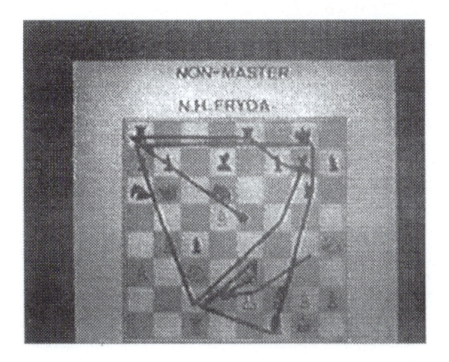

Figure 26: Eye-movements of a Non-chess-master (Analyze 1986)

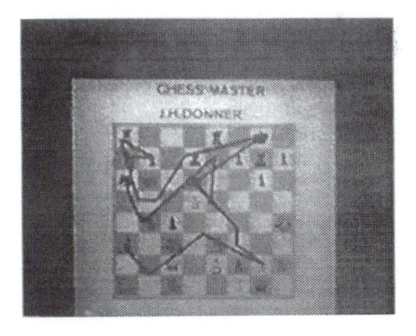

Figure 27: Eye-movements of a Chess-master (Analyze 1986)

Appendix Three: Details of Eye-Movement Recordings

The following page contains details of the eye-movement recordings described in Chapter Eight.

To illustrate the nature of the eye-movement recordings a single section from a sample recording is described here in detail. The recording is of a subject reading the subtitle illustrated on page 62 (Chapter Eight). Fixations are indicated by numbers. The time in seconds is given in brackets above each fixation. All fixations were recorded manually.

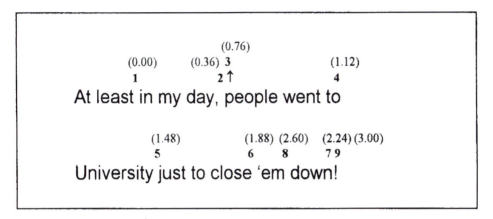

Figure 28: Three-second Sample of a Person's Eye Movements

For each subject the following measurements were taken:

- *Reading time*
Time taken to read each word (i.e. The total time on subtitle divided by the number of words (e.g. $3.00 \div 14 = 0.21$ secs per word in Figure 30).

- *Deflections*
Number of times the eyes deflected away from the subtitle area to look at the image (e.g. Once (↑3) in Figure 30).

- *Duration of Deflections*
Time between when the eye leaves and returns to the subtitle (e.g. between fixation 2 and 4 (0.76 secs) in Figure 30).

- *Regressions*
Number of times subjects re-read words or characters. (e.g. once (8) in Figure 30).

- *Re-readings*
Number of times subjects re-read the entire subtitle (e.g. 0 in Figure 30).

Appendix Four: Summary of Data on Subjects

The following page contains data on the subjects who participated in the eye-movement experiment (c.f. Chapter Eight). The data includes information on personal characteristics and reading.

Subject Data

Deaf Subjects

ID	Age	Hearing Loss (dB)	Acquisition of Sign Language (Age)
1D	38	91	5
2D	34	66-90	16
3D	29	91	0
4D	29	91	0
5D	27	91	8
6D	22	91	16
7D	24	91	3
8D	46	66-91	0
9D	43	91	20
10D	45	91	8

Table 27: Deaf Subjects: Personal Characteristics

ID	Hours of subtitled TV viewing a week	Comprehension of subtitles 1=Easy, 2=OK, 3=Hard	Reading: Material (N,M,B)* Frequency (0,1,2,3)+
1D	11-20	2	N2, M3, B0
2D	31-40 •	2	N2, M3, B3
3D	6-10 •	2	N1, M2, B3
4D	6-10 •	2	N3, M3, B2
5D	1-5	2	N2, M2, B2
6D	6-10	1	N2, M3, B1
7D	6-10	1	N3, M3, B2
8D	11-20	2	N1, M1, B1
9D	21-30	1	N2, M2, B2
10D	31-40	2	N2, M2, B0

Table 28: Deaf Subjects: Reading Data

* Reading Material: N = Newspaper, M = Magazine, B = Book
\+ Reading Frequency: 0 = Never, 1 = Rarely, 2 = Once a week, 3 = Everyday
• Plus an additional 1-9 hours of non-subtitled television, e.g. sport.

Hearing Subjects

ID	Age	Hours of TV viewing a week	Comprehension of subtitles 1=Easy, 2=OK, 3=Hard	Reading: Material (N,M,B)* Frequency (0,1,2,3)+
1H	27	0-1	1	N2, M2, B3
2H	28	11–20	1	N3, M3, B3
3H	24	0–1	2	N3, M1, B3
4H	53	1–5	1	N3, M2, B2
5H	23	1-5	2	N3, M2, B3
6H	25	6-10	1	N1, M1, B3
7H	28	0-1	1	N2, M2, B3
8H	21	1-5	1	N2, M2, B2
9H	23	6-10	1	N2, M2, B3
10H	45	11-20	1	N2, M2, B3

Table 29: Hearing Subjects: Personal Characteristics and Reading Data

* Reading Material: N = Newspaper, M = Magazine, B = Book
+ Reading Frequency: 0 = Never, 1 = Rarely, 2 = Once a week, 3 = Everyday

Bibliography

Adams M. (1979) 'Models of Word Recognition', *Cognitive Psychology* 11:133-76.

Areson A. H. and F. J. Dowaliby (1985) *Captioning for Instructional Purposes for Hearing Impaired Learners: A Review of the Literature*, Rochester: NTID.

Armstrong D., W. Stokoe and S. Wilcox (1995) *Gesture and the Nature of Language*, Cambridge: Cambridge University Press.

Ayres T. J. (1984) 'Silent Reading Time for Tongue-twister Paragraphs', *American Journal of Psychology* 97:605-609.

Bailey A. (1990) 'Good News for Deaf People', *Spectrum* 1:12-13.

Baker R. G. (1982) *Monitoring Eye-movements While Watching Subtitled Television Programmes B a Feasibility Study*, London: Independent Broadcasting Authority.

Baker R. G. (1987) 'Information Technology B A Breakthrough for Deaf People?', in J. G. Kyle (ed) *Adjustment to Acquired Hearing Loss: Analysis, Change and Learning*, Bristol: CDS, University of Bristol, 80-92.

Baker R. G., A. D. Lambourn, A. C. Downton and A. W. King (eds) (1984) *Oracle Subtitling for the Deaf and Hard of Hearing*, Southampton: Department of Electronics and Information Engineering, University of Southampton.

Baron J. and R. Treiman (1980) 'Use of Orthography in Reading and Learning to Read', in J. F. Kavanagh and R. L. Venezky (eds) *Orthography, Reading, and Dyslexia*, Baltimore: University Park Press, 120-32.

BBC (1994) *The BBC Subtitling Guide,* London: BBC.

Biber, D. (1988) *Variation across Speech and Writing*, Cambridge: Cambridge University Press.

Brien D. (ed) (1992) *Dictionary of British Sign Language/English*, London & Boston: Faber & Faber.

Buchanan C., P. Ries, P. Speielli and R. Trybus (eds) (1971) *Further Studies in Achievement Testing, Hearing Impaired Students B United States: Spring*, Washington: Gallaudet College.

Radio Times (1994) London: Chadwyck-Healey.

Cockerell, M. (1988) *Live from Number 10: The Inside Story of Prime Ministers and Television*, London: Faber & Faber.

Conrad, R. (1970) 'Short-term Processes in the Deaf', *British Journal of Psychology* 61:179-95.

------ (1971a) 'The Chronology of the Development of Covert Speech in Children', *Developmental Psychology* 5:398-405.

------ (1971b) 'The Effect of Vocalizing on Comprehension in the Profoundly Deaf', *British Journal of Psychology* 62:147-50.

------ (1972a) 'Short-term Memory in the Deaf: A Test for Speech Coding', *British Journal of Psychology* 63:173-80.

------ (1972b) 'Speech and Reading', in J. F. Kavanagh and I. Mattingly (eds) *Language by Ear and by Eye*, Cambridge, MA: MIT Press, 142-60.

------ (1973) 'Some Correlates of Speech Coding in Short-term Memory of the Deaf', *Journal of Speech and Hearing Research* 16:375-84.

------ (1977) 'The Reading Ability of Deaf School-leavers', *British Journal of Educational Psychology* 47:138-48.

------ (1979) *The Deaf Schoolchild*, London: Harper & Row.

Davies, A. C. (1989) 'The Prevalence of Hearing-impairment and Reported Hearing Disability among Adults in Great Britain', *International Journal of Epidemiology* 18:911-17.

Davison, A. and G. M. Green (eds) (1988) *Linguistic Complexity and Text Comprehension*, London: Lawrence Erlbaum Associates.

de Linde, Z. C. (1995) "Read My Lips': Subtitling Principles, Practices and Problems', *Perspectives: Studies in Translatology* 1:9-20.

------ (1996) 'Le sous-titrage intralinguistique pour les sourds et les mal entendants', in Y. Gambier (ed) *Les Transferts Linguistiques Dans Les Medias Audiovisuels*, Paris: Presses Universitaires du Septentrion, 165-83.

Desaele, F. K. Verfaillie, P. Bulckaert and G. d'Ydewalle (1992) *Ondertiteling als Taalstimulering voor Prelinguaal Doven*, Belgium: Department of Psychology, University of Leuven.

Di Francesca, S. (1972) *Academic Achievement Test Results of a National Testing Programme for Hearing-impaired Students. United States: Spring, 1971 (Report No.9, Series D)*, Washington, DC: Gallaudet College, Office of Demographic Studies.

Dodd, B. (1980) 'The Spelling Abilities of Profoundly Pre-lingually Deaf Children', in U. Frith (ed) *Cognitive Processes in Spelling*, New York & London: Academic Press, 115-35.

------ and B. Hermelin (1977) 'Phonological Coding by the Prelinguistically Deaf', *Perception and Psychophysics* 21:413-17.

d'Ydewalle, G., J. Van Rensbergen and J. Pollet (1987) 'Reading a Message When the Same Message is Available in Another Language: The Case of Subtitling', in J. K. O'Regan and A. Levy-Schoen (eds) *Eye Movements: From Physiology to Cognition*, Amsterdam: Elsevier Science Publishers.

d'Ydewalle, G., C. Praet, J. Verfaillie and J. Van Rensbergen (1988) *Choosing between Redundant Information Channels: Speech and Text (Psychological Reports No. 84)*, Belgium: Laboratory of Experimental Psychology, University of Leuven/Louvain.

d'Ydewalle, G. and J. Van Rensbergen (1989) 'Developmental Studies of Text-picture Interaction in the Perception of Animated Cartoons with Text', in H. Mandl and J. R. Levin (eds) *Knowledge Acquisition from Text and Pictures*, Amsterdam: Elsevier Science Publishers, 223-48.

d'Ydewalle, G. and I. Gielen (1992) 'Attention Allocation with Overlapping Sound, Image, and Text', in K. Rayner (ed) *Eye Movements and Visual Cognition*, New York: Springer-Verlag, 415-27.

d'Ydewalle, G. and M. Vanderbeeken (1996) *Perceptual and Cognitive Processing of Editing Rules in Film*, Leuven, Belgium: Department of Psychology.

EBU (1993) *Conference Notes*, Oslo: Norwegian Broadcasting Corporation, NRK.

Edfeldt, A. W. (1960) *Silent Speech and Silent Reading*, Chicago: University of Chicago Press.

Epee, C. M. (Abbe de L') (1784) *La Veritable Maniere D'instruire les Sourds et Muets*, Paris: Nyon L'aine.

Erickson, D., I. G. Mattingly and M. T. Turvey (1977) 'Phonetic Activity in Reading: An Experiment with Kanji', *Language and Speech* 20:384-403.

European Commission DG XIII (1995) *Background to the Workplan for the IVth Framework Programme*, Brussels: European Commission.

Ewoldt, C. (1984) 'Problems with Rewritten Materials, as Exemplified by 'To Build a Fire'', *American Annals of the Deaf* 1:23-28.

Frumkin, B. and M. Anisfeld (1977) 'Semantic and Surface Codes in the Memory of Deaf Children', *Cognitive Psychology* 9:475-93.

Gambier, Y. (1996) *Les Transferts Linguistiques dans Les Medias Audiovisuels*, Paris: Presses Universitaires du Septentrion.

Garrity, L. I. (1977) 'Electromyography: A Review of the Current Status of Subvocal Speech Research', *Memory and Cognition* 5:615-22.

Gielen, I. and G. d'Ydewalle (1992) 'How Do We Watch Subtitled Television Programmes?', in A. Demetrion, A. Efklides, E. Gonida and M. Vakali (eds) *Psychological Research in Greece: Vol.1 Development, Learning, and Instruction*, Thessaloniki: Arestotelian University Press, 247-59.

Gill, J. (1995) *The Forgotten Millions: Access to Telecommunications for People with Disabilities*, Brussels, Luxembourg: COST 219, The European Commission.

Goodman, K. S. (1970) 'Reading: A Psycholinguistic Guessing Game', *Journal of the Reading Specialist* 6:126-35.

Gottlieb, H. (1994) 'Subtitling: Diagonal Translation, *Perspectives: Studies in Translatology* 2:101-12.

Gough, P. (1972) 'One Second of Reading', in J. F. Kavanagh and I. G. Mattingly (eds) *Language by Ear and by Eye*, Cambridge MA: MIT Press.

Graddol, D. (1994) 'The Visual Accomplishment of Factuality', in D. Graddol and O. Boyd-Barett (eds) *Media Texts: Authors and Readers*, Clevedon: Multilingual Matters & The Open University, 136-57.

Graddol, D. and O. Boyd-Barett (1994) (eds) *Media Texts: Authors and Readers*, Clevedon: Multilingual Matters & The Open University,

Gregory, S. (1996) *Dial 888: Subtitling for Deaf Children*, London: Independent Television Commission.

Gunter, B. (1988) *Attitudes towards the Use of Subtitles and Sign Language Inserts for the Deaf and Hard-of-Hearing on Television*, London: Independent Broadcasting Authority.

------ (1993) *Television. The Public's View*, London: ITC.

Haber, R. N. and L. R. Haber (1982) 'Does Silent Reading Involve Articulation? Evidence from Tongue-twisters', *American Journal of Psychology* 95:409-19.

Halliday, M. A. K. (1985) *Spoken and Written Language*, Victoria: Deakin University Press.

------ (1994) 'Spoken and Written Modes of Meaning', in D. Graddol D. and O. Boyd-Barett (eds) *Media texts: Authors and Readers*, Clevedon, England: Multilingual Matters & The Open University, 51-73.

------ and R. Hasan (1976) *Cohesion in English*, Hong Kong: Longman Group Ltd.

Hammermeister, F. K. (1971) 'Reading achievement in Deaf Adults', *American Annals of the Deaf* 116:25-28.

Hardyck, C. D. and L. F. Petrinovich (1970) 'Subvocal Speech and Comprehension as a Function of Difficulty Level of Reading Material', *Journal of Verbal Learning and Verbal Behavior* 9:647-52.

Hoey, M. (1991) *Patterns of Lexis in Text*, Oxford: Oxford University Press.

Huey, E. (1908) *The Psychology and Pedagogy of Reading*, New York: Macmillan.

Humphreys, G. and L. Evett (1985) 'Are There Independent Lexical and Non-lexical Routes in Word Processing? An Evaluation of the Dual-route Theory of Reading', *Behavioral and Brain Sciences* 8:689-740.

Ignotus, P. (1972) *Hungary*, London: Ernest Benn.

ITC (1993) *ITC Guidance on Standards for Subtitling*, London: ITC.

ITC (1996) 'Good News for Deaf People', *Spectrum* 23:12-13.

ITC (1997) *News Release, Independent Television Commission*, London: ITC Press Office.

Just, M. and P. Carpenter (1980) 'A Theory of Reading: From Eye Fixations to Comprehension', *Psychological Review* 87:329-54.

Katzman, S. and D. Penkoff (1994) *Smile When You Say That: Graphic Accents as Gender Markers in Computer-Mediated Communication*, Palo Alto: Stanford University.

Kimura, Y. (1984) 'Concurrent Vocal Interference: Its Effects on Kanan and Kanji', *Quarterly Journal of Experimental Psychology* 36A:117-32.

------ and P. Bryant (1983) 'Reading and Writing in English and Japanese: A Cross-cultural Study of Young Children', *British Journal of Developmental Psychology* 1:143-54.

Kleiman, G. (1975) 'Speech Recoding in Reading', *Journal of Verbal Learning and Verbal Behavior* 14:323-39.

Kovačič, I. (1992) *Subtitling Translation B Linguistic Perspectives*, PhD Dissertation, University of Ljubljana, Slovenia.

------ (1994) 'Relevance as a Factor in Subtitling Reductions', in C. Dollerup and A. Loddegaard (eds) *Teaching Translation and Interpreting 2. Insights, Aims, Visions*, Amsterdam & Philadelphia: John Benjamins, 245-51.

Kyle, J. G. (ed) (1992) *Switched On: Deaf Peopl's Views on Television Subtitling*, Bristol: CDS, ITC, BBC.

------ and G. Pullen (1985) *Young Deaf People in Employment*, Bristol: School of Education, Bristol.

------ and B. Woll (1985) *Sign Language*, Cambridge: Cambridge University Press.

Levinson, S. (1989) 'A Review of Relevance', *Journal of Linguistics* 25:445-72.

Levy, B. (1978) 'Speech Analysis during Sentence Processing: Reading and Listening', *Visible Language* 12:81-101.

Locke, J. (1970) 'Short-term Memory Encoding Strategies in the Deaf', *Psychonomic Science* 18:233-34.

------ (1978) 'Phonemic Effects in the Silent Reading of Hearing and Deaf Children', *Cognition* 6:73-87.

------ and V. Locke (1971) 'Deaf Children's Phonetic, Visual and Dactylic Coding in a Grapheme Recall Task', *Journal of Experimental Psychology* 89:142-46.

Lodge, N. (1994) *The European AUDETEL Project B Enhancing Television for Visually Impaired People*, London: IEE Colloquium on Information Access for People with Disability.

London, J. (1968) 'To Build a Fire', in J. London (ed) *Adventures in Appreciation*, New York: Harcourt, Brace & World, 1-15.

Luyken, G. M., T. Herbst, J. Langham-Brown, H. Reid and H. Spinhof (1991) *Overcoming Language Barriers in Television*, Manchester: The European Institute for the Media.

Marleau, L. (1980) 'Les sous-titres un mal necessaire', *Meta* 27(3):271-85.

Martin, M. (1972) 'Nonalphabetic Writing Systems: Some Observations', in J. Kavanagh and I. Mattingly (eds) *Language by Ear and by Eye*, Cambridge, MA: MIT Press.

Masterman, L. (1980) *Teaching About Television*, London: Macmillan.

Mattingley, I. (1972) 'Reading, the Linguistic Process, and Linguistic Awareness', in J. Kavanagh and I. Mattingley (eds) *Language by Ear and by Eye*, Cambridge, MA: MIT Press, .

McClelland, J. L. (1986) 'The Programmable Blackboard Model of Reading', in J. L. McClelland, D. E. Rumelhart and PDP Research Group (eds) *Parallel Distributed Processing: Explorations in the Microstructure of Cognition. Vol. II*, Cambridge MA: Bradford Books.

McGuigan, F. (1971) 'External Auditory Feedback from Covert Oral Behavior during Silent Reading', *Psychonomic Science* 25:212-14.

------ and S. Bailey (1969) 'Longitudinal Study of Covert Oral Behavior during Silent Reading', *Perceptual and Motor Skills* 28:170.

Minchinton, J. (1993) *Sub-Titling*, Hertfordshire, England: J. Minchinton.

Nida, E. (1969) *Toward a Science of Translating*, Leiden: Brill.

Norwood, M. (1988) *The Development and Growth of Closed Captioned Television*, El Paso, Texas: National Conference on Deaf and Hard of Hearing People.

Nunan, D. (1993) *Discourse Analysis*, London: Penguin Group.

Padmore, D. (1994) *Language in the Multicultural Community*, MA Thesis, BBC.

Praet, C., K. Verfaillie, P. De Graef, J. Van Rensbergen and G. d'Ydewalle (1990) 'A One Line Text is Not Half a Two Line Text', in R. Groner, G. d'Ydewalle and R. Parham (eds) *From Eye to Mind: Information Acquisition in Perception, Search and Reading*, Amsterdam: Elsevier Science Publishers, 205-13.

Quigley, S. P. (1984) *Language and Deafness*, San Diego, California: College-Hill Press.

Quinn, L. (1981) 'Reading Skills of Hearing and Congenitally Deaf Children', *Journal of Experimental Child Psychology* 32:139-61.

Rayner, K. and A. Pollatsek (1989) *The Psychology of Reading,* New Jersey: Prentice-Hall.

Reid, H. (1991) 'Linguistic Problems Associated with Subtitling', in G. M. Luyken, T. Herbst, J. Langham-Brown, H. Reid and H. Spinhof *Overcoming Language Barriers in Television*, Manchester: The European Institute for the Media, 156-58.

Richards, J., J. Platt and H. Weber (1985) *Longman Dictionary of Applied Linguistics*, Hong Kong: Longman.

Russell, M. (1976) *Linguistics and Deaf Children*, Washington DC: Alexander Graham Bell Association.

Seidenberg, M. (1985) 'Constraining Models of Word Recognition', *Cognition* 20:169-90.

Shand, M. (1982) 'Sign-based Short-term Coding of American Sign Language Signs and Printed English Words by Congenitally Deaf Signers', *Cognitive Psychology* 14:1-12.

Shroyer, E. H. and J. Birch (1980) 'Captions and Reading Rates of Hearing Impaired Students', *American Annals of the Deaf* 125(7):916-22.

Simpson, J. A. and E. S. C. Weiner (eds) (1989) *The Oxford English Dictionary*, Oxford: Clarendon Press.

Slowiaczek, M. and C. Clifton (1980) 'Subvocalization and Reading for Meaning', *Journal of Verbal Learning and Verbal Behavior* 19:573-82.

Sokolov, A. (1872) *Inner Speech and Thought*, New York: Plenum.

Sperber, D. and D. Wilson (1986) *Relevance: Communication and Cognition*, Oxford: Basil Blackwell.

Stokoe, W. C. (1978) *Sign Language Structure*, Silver Spring MD: Linstok.

------, D. Casterline and C. Groneberg (eds) (1965) *A Dictionary of American Sign Language*, Washington, DC: Gallaudet College Press.

Sutton-Spence, R. (1995) *Finger-Spelling*, PhD Dissertation, Bristol: CDS, University of Bristol.

Technology Assessment Program (1993) Washington DC: Gallaudet Research Institute.

Taylor, I. and M. Taylor (1983) *The Psychology of Reading*, New York: Academic Press.

Thorn, S. (1990) *The Tenth Anniversary of the National Captioning Institute: Getting the Word Out for Ten Years*, Falls Church, VA: National Captioning Institute News.

Titford, C. (1982) 'Sub-Titling B Constrained Translation', *Lebende Sprachen* 27(3):113-16.

Tosi, V., L. Mecacci and E. Pasquali. (1994) *Movimenti Oculari e Percezione il Sequenze Filmiche*, Rome, Italy: Centro Sperimentale di Cinematografia.

Toury, G. (1980) 'Translated Literature: System, Norm, Performance: Toward a TT-oriented Approach to Literary Translation', in G. Toury *In Search of a Theory of Translation*, Tel Aviv: The Porter Institute for Poetics and Semiotics, 35-50.

Treiman, R., J. Baron and K. Luk (1981) 'Speech Recoding in Silent Reading: A Comparison of Chinese and English', *Journal of Chinese Linguistics* 9:116-24.

Treiman, R. and K. Hirsh-Pasek (1983) 'Silent Reading: Insights from Second-generation Deaf Readers', *Cognitive Psychology* 15:39-65.

Trybus, R. and M. Karchmer (1977) 'School Achievement Scores of Hearing Impaired Children: National Data on Achievement Status and Growth Patterns', *American Annals of the Deaf* 122:62-69.

Turner, G. (1994) 'Film Language', in D. Graddol and O. Boyd-Barett (eds) *Media Texts: Authors and Readers*, Clevedon: Multilingual Matters and The Open University, 119-65.

Tzeng, O. and D. Hung (1980) 'Reading in a Non-alphabetic Writing System', in J. Kavanagh and R. Venezky (eds) *Orthography, Reading and Dyslexia*, Baltimore: University Park Press.

------ and W. Wang (1977) 'Speech Recoding in Reading Chinese Characters', *Journal of Experimental Psychology: Human Learning and Memory* 3:621-30.

Van Cleve, J. (ed) (1987) *Gallaudet Encyclopaedia of Deaf People and Deafness*, New York: McGraw-Hill Book Company.

Van Orden, G. (1987) 'A Rows is a Rose: Spelling, Sound, and Reading', *Memory and Cognition* 15:181-98.

Vaughan, D. (1976) *Television Documentary Usage*, London: British Film Institute, Monograph 6.

Verfaillie, K. and G. d'Ydewalle (1987) *Modality Preference and Message Comprehension in Deaf Youngsters Watching TV (Psychological Reports No. 70)*, Leuven, Belgium: Laboratory of Experimental Psychology, University of Leuven.

Webster, A. (1986) *Deafness, Development and Literacy*, London: Methuen & Co.

Woll, B. (1991) *Sign Language on Television*, Bristol: CDS, University of Bristol.

------, J. Kyle and M. Deuchar (1981) *Perspectives on British Sign Language and Deafness*, Oxford: Biling and Sons.

Yik, W. (1978) 'The Effect of Visual and Acoustic Similarity on Short-term Memory for Chinese Words', *Quarterly Journal of Experimental Psychology* 30:487-94.

List of films

Analyse (1986) *Analyse*, Netherland: De Wetenschappelijke Film.
BBC1 (1994) *Absolutely Fabulous*, London: BBC1.
BBC1 (1994) *EastEnders*, London: BBC1.
BBC1 (1994) *Home Truths*, London: BBC1.
BBC1 (1994) *How Do They Do That?*, London: BBC1.
BBC2 (1994) *Horizon*, London: BBC2.
BBC2 (1994) *In Search of Our Ancestors*, London: BBC2.
Channel Four (1994) *Brookside*, London: Channel Four.
Channel Four (1994) *Oprah Winfrey*, London: Channel Four.
HTV (1994) *News*, London: HTV.

Index

Related Titles Available from St. Jerome

Translating for the Media
Edited by Yves Gambier

A collection of twenty-five papers covering a variety of topics relating to language transfer. Issues addressed include language challenges in the new media landscape, commercial videos, the training of screen translators, and much else.

320 pp. 1998. Pb. £24.50/$43 inc. postage and packing

Language Transfer and Audiovisual Communication. A Bibliography
Edited by Yves Gambier

New Edition containing 1300 entries, dating mainly from 1975 to 1997. Lists works on language transfer irrespective of form (dubbing, subtitling, voice over, interpreting) and context (cinema, radio, television, opera, theatre).

102pp, 1997, Pb. £11.75/$20.50, inc. postage and packing

On Translating French Literature & Film
Edited by Geoffrey Harris

A collection of essays on literary and screen translation which project translation as a complex creative task and demonstrate the authorial credentials of the translator.

227pp. 1996. Pb. £16.50/$29, inc. postage and packing

Dubbing and Subtitling: Guidelines for Production and Distribution
Josephine Dries

Producers and distributors of films and television programmes are often too unfamiliar with the subtitling and/or dubbing procedure to foresee potential problems. These guidelines have been put together to show producers and distributors how they can take language transfer into account in developing their productions.

73pp. 1995. Pb. £17.25/$31, inc. postage and packing

Overcoming Language Barriers in Television. Dubbing and Subtitling for the European Audience
Georg-Michael Luyken, with Thomas Herbst, Jo Langham-Brown, Helen Reid & Herman Spinhof

A detailed analysis of the European market for language transfer, covering methods of transfer in the audiovisual field, effects on the audience, costs, the potential of new developments, and the skills required for language transfer. Essential reading for audiovisual translators, broadcasting professionals, programme makers and policy makers.

213pp. 1991. Pb. £21.50/$38, inc. postage and packing

New Titles from St. Jerome

Translating Cultures
An Introduction for Translators, Interpreters and Mediators
David Katan
ISBN 1-900650-14-2
270 pp. 1999. Pb. £25.50/$44.50 inc. postage and packing

Translation in a Postcolonial Context
Early Irish Literature in English Translation
Maria Tymoczko
ISBN 1-900650-16-9
320 pp. 1999. Pb. £22.50/$39.50 inc. postage and packing

Unity in Diversity
Current Trends in Translation Studies
Edited by Lynne Bowker, Michael Cronin, Dorothy Kenny and Jennifer Pearson
ISBN 1-900650-15-0
208 pp. 1998. Pb. £24/$42 inc. postage and packing

Translation and Language Teaching
Language Teaching and Translation
Edited by Kirsten Malmkjær
ISBN 1-900650-17-7
160 pp. 1998. Pb. £19.50/$34 inc. postage and packing

Translation and Minority
Special Issue of *The Translator* (Volume 4/2, 1998)
Guest-edited by Lawrence Venuti
ISBN 1-900650-10-X
260 pp. 1998. Pb. £30/$52.50 inc. postage and packing

Bibliography of Translation Studies
Compiled by Lynne Bowker, Dorothy Kenny and Jennifer Pearson
ISBN 1-900650-13-4
132 pp. December 1998 (first edition). Pb. £15/$26.50, inc. postage and packing

Translation in Systems
Descriptive and System-oriented Approaches Explained
Theo Hermans
ISBN 1-900650-1-8
140 pp. 1999. Pb. £19.50/$34 inc. postage and packing

The Translator
Studies in Intercultural Communication

Published as one volume of two issues per year
(approximately 260 pages, April and November)
ISSN 1355-6509
Available from St. Jerome Publishing

A refereed international journal that publishes articles on a variety of issues related to translation and interpreting as acts of intercultural communication, without restriction in scope to any particular school of thought or academic group. *The Translator* aims to provide a meeting point for existing as well as future approaches and to stimulate interaction between various groups who share a common concern for translation as a profession and translation studies as a discipline. *Translation* is understood to cover all types of translation, whether written or oral, including activities such as literary and commercial translation, various forms of oral interpreting, dubbing, voice-overs, subtitling, translation for the stage, and such under-researched areas as sign language interpreting and community interpreting.

Annual Subscription Rates (Volume 5, 1999)

	UK	Europe	Other
Institution	£54/$94	£56/$98	£58/$101
Individual	£30/$52.50	£32/$56	£34/$59.50

All prices are inclusive of postage and packing. Back issues are available on request.

Translation Studies Abstracts

Published as one volume of two issues per year
(approximately 192 pages, June and December)
ISSN 1460-3063. Available from St. Jerome Publishing

TSA is a new initiative designed to provide a major and unique research tool, primarily for scholars of translation and interpreting. It is the first abstracting service of its kind, focusing on and covering all aspects of research within the domain of translation studies, including translation theory, interpreting, history of translation, process-oriented studies, corpus-based studies, translation and gender, translation and cultural identity, translator training/pedagogy, translation policies, bible/religious translation, literary translation, screen translation, technical & legal translation, machine (-aided) translation, terminology, community/dialogue interpeting, conference interpreting, court interpreting, and signed language interpreting.

Translation studies has many points of contact with other disciplines, especially linguistics, pragmatics, comparative literature, cultural studies, gender studies, postcolonial studies, corpus linguistics, anthropology, ethnography, and any field of study concerned with the history of ideas. Scholars working in any of these fields will find much of direct relevance in *TSA*.

TSA Editor: Maeve Olohan, UMIST, UK

Consulting Editors:
Andrew Chesterman (Finland)
Birgitta Englund Dimitrova (Sweden)
Adolpho Gentile (Australia)
Theo Hermans (UK)
Rosa Rabádan (Spain)
Ronald Sim (Kenya)
Gideon Toury (Israel)
Maria Tymoczko (USA)

Subscription to Volume 2 (1999)
Institutional: £62/$109(UK & Europe) / £65/$114 (Outside Europe), inc postage & packing
Individual: £32/$56 (UK & Europe) / £35/$62 (Outside Europe), inc. postage & packing

Bibliography of Translation Studies (Companion to *TSA*)
ISBN 1-900650-13-4

Available free for subscribers to *TSA*
Price for non-subscribers: £15/$26.50, inc. postage & packing